How to Love Your Wife

——— J. A. Myers ———

PALMETTO
PUBLISHING
Charleston, SC
www.PalmettoPublishing.com

How to Love Your Wife
Copyright © 2023 by J. A. Myers

All rights reserved

No portion of this book may be reproduced, stored in a retrieval system, or transmitted in any form by any means–electronic, mechanical, photocopy, recording, or other–except for brief quotations in printed reviews, without prior permission of the author.

Paperback ISBN: 979-8-8229-2779-7

Acknowledgements

Romans 8:28 is the first of my acknowledgments. I acknowledge I am imperfect, and my mistakes can help other men become better Christians, husbands, and fathers. Mistakes serve two purposes: they can be your undertaker or your teacher; it all depends on you. Do you beat yourself up on things you cannot change, or do you take the lesson as a learning experience and work not to repeat it?

I acknowledge great people who, without them, my life may have been more difficult than ever. I recognize the need for a spiritual father, Pastor Woodall, thank you for all you have done, are doing, and will do. Thank you for your heart.

Pastor Harris, thank you for all you do. Words cannot describe your heart, so I will not try. You genuinely show Jesus, and for that, thank you; it makes taking your orders easy.

Mitch Glenn... Wow! You are so much of a father, brother, friend, and provide great ears. You listened and never judged: you heard, felt, and then said, "Let's go eat Chinese food." You showed you understood God, and I thank Him for placing you in my life. Thanks for all you are.

Henry Thomas, thank you. With your encouragement, I took the steps to publish the first book and this one. Thank you for being my friend.

Mom... All I will say is thank you. It goes higher than you can imagine and lower than you can believe.

Table of Contents

Acknowledgements iii
Introduction 1
Fallacies of Marriage 6
   Fallacy 1:" Happy Wife, Happy Life." 7
   Fallacy 2: "Being the strong, tough husband." 8
   Fallacy 3: "Proving love through gifts." 9
   Fallacy 4: We will both lead the family together, 50/50 Leadership. 10
   Fallacy 5: Keeping families out of our business. 11
   Fallacy 6: I can still hang out with my friends like before 12
Establishing a Personal Relationship with God 13
Loving Your Wife 15
I Married an Adult 17
The Over Apologetic Husband 20
Being Her Calm 22
Boundaries 24
TESTED 27
Rejection 35
Fear of Failure 37
Buy a Suit 43
The Argument 45
Be Better Than You Were Yesterday 50
The Yellow Sticky 52
Go Stand in the Corner 55
T.R.A.P 59

The Blind Side	63
Listening Rather than Solving	67
Understanding Your Wife	70
Pay Yourself	73
The Blended Family	76
Intimacy vs Sex	79
Practice Self-Care	83
Loving At the Door	84
The Real Man	88
Doing Things Together, I Miss You	91
Sick and Tired of Being Sick and Tired	94

Introduction

Interestingly, many women enter marriages assuming they know all the rules, or at least most of them believe they do. They seem well-versed in the ins and outs of marriage and relationships, or at least the parts that benefit them. Conversely, men barely know anything about marriage, getting to the altar, and beyond. Men hear bits and pieces of information on marriage. Who provides this information? Women. They inform their husbands how to act, handle money, raise kids, and what friends are acceptable. Women even break down how a REAL MAN is supposed to act. Really? How did this happen? I really want to know. HOW DID THIS HAPPEN? When did women become experts on what it takes for MEN to be men, husbands, and fathers? When did men readily adopt their advice given as the golden rule?

Women use the phrase Real Men to belittle or magnify their man's shortcomings. This is designed to shake men up, change, or gain control over them. Where does this behavior come from? The answer is simple. In most cases, this behavior stems from homes where the absence of a man is felt and missing in the lives of their sons? Having a man in the house allows young men to learn how to be men, do what men do, say what men say or don't say, and, most importantly, learn how men worship.

Each young man's journey is different, but the lessons are the same. Individually, they will have opportunities to learn how to treat women, how husbands should treat their wives, and what to look for, expect, or require when searching for them. Husbands can learn how to distinguish what woman deserves to wear the title of his last name. If he is lucky, the woman he finds will be worthy of the sacrifices, blood, sweat, and even his tears. He will realize that he is a precious prize worthy of a good thing. He learns how to grow into the role of honor, character, and integrity. He understands how to be a man by watching a man every day.

Without a man in the house, the boy learns manhood from the woman and grasps things the woman's way, which is totally different from a man's. He mimics her behavior, her attitude, and her strengths. What's wrong with that? A lot! The issue is that he needs to learn more about himself and how to become the man he is supposed to be. He becomes accustomed to going to her when he has problems. She becomes his fixer, leaving him with little knowledge of overcoming struggles or adversities alone. Eventually, he believes he should rely on her to handle his money because she's better at it. Quickly and silently, he adapts to understanding that the woman controls the finances in the house and thus controls the home. Subconsciously, he allows himself to believe her way is better; I'm not good with these types of things. Instead of doing the work to see if he could, he falls into a routine of giving her 95 percent of his money and asking her for some of it back when he wants or needs it. For some reason, he feels guilty for taking something he worked for from her. He remembers how his Mama solved everything, so why should he try? Mama was the original fixer who would bail him out of any situation and then blamed the system, the world, for his inability to try, lead, and forge through. He learns it's okay to QUIT. Once quitting starts, it takes off at full speed. He leaves jobs, teams, friends, and intimate relationships and finally ... gives up on himself.

Thus, in many marriages, a conflict may arise between the new wife and his mother, each vying to control the new husband and the old son. The mother wants to protect him from any hurt, harm, or danger that she feels may change her love (control) over him, while the wife wants to show him how to break that control and become a leader in their marriage and home. If he is not confident in his decision-making process, he will lose his wife and mother. He may need to learn how to transition into his new role as a husband while still maintaining his original position as a son. BOOM! There is a significant chance that a fight for control will erupt from this conflict unless he can figure out a way to appease them both. He could potentially lose his marriage because neither his wife nor mother are willing to accept his manhood, and he doesn't know how to show or use it. As a child, he had no man to teach him how to transition from boy… to young man… to man.

Marriage is the second most important decision a man will make; accepting Christ is the first. This shows how important marriage is in God's design. It's not something to be entered into lightly or crazily but with certainty and soberly. Before pursuing, ponder this: it is not a 50/50 relationship. It is a relationship in which he will step in as the leader and must be prepared to handle all that is involved. Genesis 2:18 says, "It is not good for man to be alone." Proverbs 18:22 says, "He who finds a wife finds a good thing and obtains favor from the Lord." Choosing a bride, when, and where to get married should include being as ready as possible for every situation. The only way to do this is for him to be the best man he can be daily. Marriage has a way of presenting surprises, shock, and amazement to every husband. Yes, EVERY husband.

When it comes to her, he should consider these questions:
- Is she a wife? Is she emotionally ready to become his wife?
- Is she a helpmate?

Most importantly...
- What is her relationship with God?

As a couple, he should contemplate how he would answer these questions:
- Can he... lead this woman?
- Will he... lead her?
- Will she... follow him?

Many memories are created in a marriage, some good and some not. These memories last for a lifetime and are designed for husbands and wives to share stories of them meeting, falling in love, things they did, places they went, and especially tales of the birth of their children. Marriage is also designed to help them both handle the loss of family members, friends, and other situations God has allowed to happen in their lives. Husbands and wives help each other heal and be open. They help each other be normal and love. These memories are for husbands and wives and require work to ensure a successful marriage. They should not be locked away or recreated with another, then another, and yet another. Therefore, the decision-making process in choosing a wife is essential and personal. It should not be done under pressure or force from others advising on how good a wife she will make (Side note: they offer their definition of who has the potential to be YOUR wife) or look at how much money she has. Material things can build a house, but they rarely make a home.

When choosing a wife, there must be accountability in the marriage. To WHOM is marriage accountable? A marriage cannot be the responsibility of two imperfect people: husband and wife. It must be responsible to perfection, God. The husband and wife must be equally yoked, having the same God who designed the marriage. This is more important than beauty, charm, and finances.

If they are not equally yoked and do not worship the same God, they may face in-law problems and risk being controlled by two different fathers. This book will provide hope, encouragement, and insights using Biblical examples on how to handle different situations when they occur. Not if… but when. Let's go.

Fallacies of Marriage

Men realize, sooner or later, in a marriage, they don't know how to be a husband. They fall prey to believing what they see on television, read in novels, or what is shared by others is all there is to marriage. Realistically, this can be far from the truth and have negative consequences. As the saying goes, "Don't believe the hype." Bride and groom say their vows, enjoy a romantic honeymoon, have plenty of sex, (hopefully) then return home in hopes of a happily ever after. This is where everything works perfectly…right? The two are now one. He knows there will be issues but believes with his new bride, they can work through these issues together. Did he consider what that anything is and how long it will last? Now, he realizes no one taught him what to expect, what to do, or even how to feel. Since no one taught him how to be a husband, he may feel it is unnecessary. He may use Phillip Banks (Uncle Phil on Fresh Prince) or James Evans (father on Good Times) to model his behavior after. It's just a role he jumps into and makes work, right? No biggie. It's as smooth as going from one grade to another, one school to another, or one girl to another. Too simple. He may think he knows marriage and ask, "What can be all that tough about it? We've known each other for a long time, and click; we have no problems we cannot solve?"

Now he is married with a wife, so… what's next? How does he live? His everyday life is GONE; he has new roles to learn and must figure out things quickly. How does he become a husband who will make God and his family proud? How does he love his wife the way God would want? Like many men, he is trying to figure out how to love their wives and please God at the same time. Yes, it is possible. Before we go any further, let's tackle a few fallacies about marriage.

Fallacy 1:" Happy Wife, Happy Life."
Where this came from is a mystery to me, but this fallacy has several problems. What makes a wife happy is something men and women have been trying to solve from as far back as Adam. What makes her happy today may not make her happy tomorrow, especially if she is going through emotional, hormonal, or physical changes. Mood changes like these often leave husbands wondering if they did something wrong, or if they are incompetent, or worse... a failure as a husband. A husband doing nice things for his wife is not wrong...but if he is doing them to win her love or keep her "happy," it may give her control over the relationship and could reverse the plans of God for their marriage. It may also bring on feelings of being used and cause the husband to question God's plan for the marriage. Following this fallacy may cause a loss of respect for the marriage and each other. When respect for the marriage is lost or trying to be won, the husband is no longer honest with himself or with their marriage. He believes he is not good at being a husband and may soon begin trying to act the part. Not knowing who will show up the next day, the representative, the husband, or the actor, becomes frustrating.

This fallacy creates a kind leader rather than a leader who is kind. The difference is the priority of leadership. A kind leader has lost focus on being the leader God wants him to be. His decisions are based on being kind and fearing hurting his wife's feelings; thus, he gives little to no input, or worse… his wife makes decisions for him. She picks out everything, from homes, cars, churches, schools, and even his clothes. Not that these are wrong, but he has little to no say in any of these decisions. Worst of all, he is okay with this way of leadership; he does not want to hurt her feelings, and he does not want to tell her no. He even allows her to walk outside him as they walk down the street, as if she is now protecting him rather than him protecting her.

Leaders who are kind make decisions not with arrogance or cockiness; they do it politely, firmly, and confidently. They answer with love and realize decisions must be completed and made. This leadership shows the wife that love and kindness are in decision-making. It shows her she has a man who she can build trust in, one who is confident in making decisions, and one she can follow and put her strength in supporting. It allows her to let go because her husband has control and knows how to use it. He is not a kind leader, but a leader who is kind. He makes the decisions and implements them.

Fallacy 2: "Being the strong, tough husband."
This is the husband who seems unbothered, calm, or unfazed by anything. He portrays the image of not feeling hurt. He is perceived as the husband whose wife can stay or go. He is stuck in the mindset of "This is my house, my rules" type of husband. He's the boss head honcho and has the final say on everything. Anyone who defies him risks suffering the consequences for defying his rules. He accuses his wife of betrayal, lying, hiding, and listening to the wrong friends. Constantly telling her to leave her friends alone, even down to quitting her job, for he has something better for her to do. He wants to isolate her, make her only available to him and his way of thinking. This… is wrong. It's not God's way; it lacks respect for himself, his wife, and the marriage. He is a bully, whether he realizes it or not. His attitude damages his wife's emotions, thinking, and the marriage. Thinking and behaving

this way makes his wife afraid of him and causes her to change how she responds. She responds more out of fear than out of love. She will not be the woman or wife she could be. Instead, she may become a wife of fear, worry, and low self-esteem, ready to escape his presence and grasp. He will complain about sex or the lack of sex because she is no longer turned on by him and follows through the motions; she has lost her feel for intimacy. He has not read Proverbs 31, Woman.

Fallacy 3: "Proving love through gifts."
This is covered briefly in the first fallacy, but I want to elaborate further. This means a husband loves his wife by providing her with material things (i.e., cars, houses, jewelry, clothes) or anything he believes will ensure her love stays in place or grows for him. These actions may become unrealistic and damaging to their romance, finances, and marriage. He becomes more of a "Sugar Daddy" and less of a husband. This is an excellent example of the "Kind Leader." Is it wrong? No, but gifts can't replace the leadership, structure, and discipline a husband provides. Material things are not a substitute for love. A husband should be sought out for the great things he can provide: integrity, honor, character, leadership, and love.

This fallacy turns the marriage into a show marriage, allowing people to look and wonder what trinket was purchased this time or envy how so much love is displayed in that marriage. Ooh, look… what will he buy her next? They say that marriage is extraordinary and coveted. It's a lot of pressure to convince people of a happy marriage when it is only based on material things and debt. Yes, especially debt; there will be lots of debt if he lives under this fallacy. Debt adds so much pressure to the marriage that it makes it difficult to enjoy the marriage and even each other. A husband is a representative of his Heavenly Husband, Jesus Christ (he is the bride of Christ). So, each husband has an example to follow; just leave out the walking on water thing for now.

Fallacy 4: We will both lead the family together, 50/50 Leadership.

Many people say and believe that in a marriage, the leadership should be 50/50: partners, co-equal, equally accountable. This is true to an extent in spirituality, but like in a business, a leader must make the final decisions, good, bad, or indifferent. That person makes the decisions and sets the organization's direction and personality. If husband and wife have equal shares, and there is a disagreement left or right, up or down, do or don't, the marriage will have problems moving forward. Someone must make the final call, someone must decide, and everyone must agree that this person is the final authority. The fallacy of 50/50 leadership cannot exist in a marriage. Making decisions together is excellent; God delegates authority to the husband. The husband does not have to make all the decisions but will be held accountable for his family. So, the husband must pay attention to his role. Husbands who give away their decision-making abilities and authority usually find it difficult to regain them.

Fallacy 5: Keeping families out of our business.

Get real. Many couples are told this as they enter their new relationship, but I am not sure they can, and I am not sure why they will want to follow this advice.

There is nothing wrong, to an extent, in allowing families into their business. They are there to help, regardless of how they put it. They are the backbone of the new family and will be needed in many ways to help the couple grow as a family. It is difficult to keep family out of relationships, especially new ones, then turn around and ask them for help. Couples should remind each other what subjects are off limits with family, friends, and kids, especially if it may cause them to take sides. The same standards the new family set may be the standards their kids set for them.

Allowing family members to give advice gives husbands and wives more options to resolve issues. It is like learning from other people's mistakes, and it helps the in-laws bond and becomes a healing part of the new marriage. Remember, couples are not required to follow any advice they are given. They should listen, receive what works for them, and eliminate what doesn't.

It takes a family to save a marriage; that family is more than just the husband and wife. Family, all of them, help the new marriage grow and survive. Every husband should take care in telling his wife to keep her family out of the marriage. She may go to this place for help, guidance, and support. It is her structure, her history, and her foundation. Receiving advice from family is okay; what is done with this advice is up to the couple. The more information, the better the decision. Keeping family out of your marriage is like having a car no one can touch, but when the car breaks down, all those who cannot handle it are called to help fix it. So, listen, learn, receive, eliminate, and then decide what advice the family will use.

Fallacy 6: I can still hang out with my friends like before

Many men believe that they can still hang out with their friends, go to the same places, and do the same things when they are married. They forget their wife now takes the place of their best friend and requires more attention than any best friend they may have. Once married, a new mindset must take place. I am a married man; I am a husband. I have a wife, and she is my top priority. Her welfare, security, and very essence now fall under my authority. Friends and family must understand this. If not, they are not invested in you or your relationship as they should be.

The wife is now her husband's best friend, and he should start treating her as that. It will not be as easy as it sounds, but as they bonded with those former friends, they can now connect with their wives. Yes, it is a two-way street; she must put forth the same effort to be his best friend as he sets forth in becoming hers. Best friends have disagreements and differences; they have issues, but in most cases, they forgive and move on. Let her know this is the goal of the new family: to be each other's best friend as much as possible, not to take the place of the old best friend. Simply becoming the new best friend. It's a growing process. Begin by discussing little things with each other, letting the relationship grow. Take part in hobbies together. This can help each other understand the other's likes and dislikes. Best friends put in the work necessary to become best friends.

Learn to put in the work.

Establishing a Personal Relationship with God

Allow God to be what He's always wanted to be: the marriage and family leader. It's crucial to allow Him to be up close and intimately connected to both husband and wife. Couples should seek Him out for all the decisions they will make. God formed them with a personal touch and breathed life into them. He opened the door for husbands to develop a relationship with Him so intense and unique that it would flow through to his wife. God made a point by creating all the animals before He created woman, man's suitable companion. She was created from the side of man, not the front nor the rear. He loves her the same. The Bible tells us that God is Love; Notice the word love, not lust. A husband's goal should be to love God first (deeper than anyone and anything) and then love his wife. God provides simple answers to every relationship; they just may not be easy. Allow Him to be God in the marriage, not just in the wedding.

A husband must do vital things, not just physically but internally. These intense things will involve improving character, integrity, and honor. Believing in God's way of guiding the family is a firm stance that must be made and held firm to, regardless of the consequences, because God is in control. Sometimes, the husband following God's guidance will go against the grain or popular opinion of friends and family. His decisions and leadership must be made without fear of consequences from the wife, family, or others getting upset because they disagree.

The closer the relationship is with God, the greater the communication is with Him. His voice is more transparent and better understood. A growing relationship with God increases self-worth, contentment, and satisfaction in His plan, especially in molding. The molding process is where He molds the husband to be better, and through the husband, He also sets the wife. This is a challenging process, but it is well worth it. It is a maturing process in which God is always there to strengthen and guide. He is removing the mess from the lives of both. A significant part of maturing is knowing God is there and trusting in the plan, no matter how it appears. He will not leave you.

Loving Your Wife

Ephesians 5:28-29 says, "Husbands love your wives as Christ loved the church and gave himself up for her. Husbands should love their wives as their own bodies; he who loves his wife loves himself." Think about it. If a husband loves himself, not out of an inflated ego, pride, or some outstanding achievement, yet truly knows who he is and whose he is, it will make it easier to love who God has made him to be. A better relationship with Christ allows a husband to show love and grace to his wife. She will need it.

One way of doing this is through worship. Joshua 24:15 (NIV), but for me and my house, we will serve the Lord. A husband should establish worship with and for his family. The husband, wife, and family should worship under one God, one leadership, and, hopefully, in one church. This is not to say two different churches won't work; it just makes it easier for the family and the worship process in and out of the house. It doesn't matter what church is attended, the wife's or the husband's; so, God should be sought in that decision. Worshiping together reduces many issues in the marriage, allows both to become closer to one accord and can discuss what took place in church and how they view what was said or done. It also allows the church to bond with the new family; the church gets to know the family, and the family gets to know the church.

A husband must have personal time to pray for his wife and family. Holding her/them in his arms each day, especially before leaving the house, and praying for her adds more emphasis on who the family serves. A wife should hear her husband tell God how thankful he is for her and how he wants God to bless her. When a husband covers his wife in prayer and love, he protects and encourages her. He should pray for better romance, finances, health, jobs, families, and anything she or the family may need. The Bible says the fervent prayers of the righteous availeth much. Therefore, husbands should make this a daily routine. A great insight into being a better husband is constantly asking God how to be a better husband and leader of the family. As God's child, he can ask Him anything. What a great Father.

In 1st Kings chapter 3, God appeared to King Solomon in a dream by night and said, "Ask what I shall give thee." Solomon had no idea how to be King and could have asked God for anything. Instead, he asked God for an understanding heart to judge Thy people between good and evil. God responded to Solomon by granting him more than he asked for. Being a husband is not easy and will require all a husband has to offer. A relationship built on the foundation with God, the designer of the Covenant, the Creator, and His Son's guidance through the maze of life is a must.

A husband should pick a place without distractions to meet God daily. This will be his holy place because God is there, just as He was with Moses. He will be with him. He should use this time to ask, talk, and give praise for what He has, is, and will do. Take time to listen. This place can be in the car (no radio), bathroom, or even a closet. It will be difficult because the enemy will try to interrupt or stop this meeting. Most men do this early in the mornings; even King David did his praying in the morning hours. Jesus did his also. It was His time to talk to His Father away from everyone, even the disciples. So, follow the excellent examples and set up a place and time to speak to God. He will show up and talk. Be prepared to sit and listen.

I Married an Adult

In marriage, it's easy to forget the person on the other side of you, the one you married, is an adult. Seriously, it happens. In many relationships, one person begins to treat the other as someone they own, control, or direct rather than an adult they married. Their conversation, tone, and attitude fluctuate from kindness to rudeness. Demands are made that are unbearable, frustrating, and somewhat degrading. If not both, one is treated as one of the kids rather than an adult. The role of a leader or helpmate is no longer valued, appreciated, or respected. No one wants to be around the other, and intimacy is damaged.

Some signs will show the relationship has or is changing; however, it does not have to stay that way. If both are willing to do the work, there is still time to turn the situation around. The first sign that a husband no longer treats his wife as an adult is when orders are given on what she can and cannot do. She can't go here or there; she can't watch this or do that. This behavior slowly places the one giving orders in a parental position and the other in a child position. He must remember he is her husband, not her father, and she, his wife, is an adult, too. Treat her as such, trust her to make adult decisions, take adult actions, and receive adult consequences. As a husband, his wife trusts him to not become her father but to remain her husband, to not dictate her every move, emotion, or expression.

Another sign is telling her which friends she can have. Let adults be adults. Let her pick her friends; she should allow her husband to do the same. Adults let adults know how things hurt or bother them, not forcing them to make changes by issuing demands. Tell her how you feel about her friends and how you will limit your time around them. When asked to disassociate with certain friends, adults tend to find similar new friends with similar characteristics, if not worse. The more complicated a husband is…, the closer the two (her and her friends) may become, making him the third wheel in the friendship/relationship. Give the concern to God and let Him address the situation.

Although there are many other signs to look for, remember you are also an adult. Be an adult in the marriage. This means asking yourself, would an adult do this? Would an adult behave this way? Would an adult treat his wife this way? If you treat her as a child, why would she want to be around you? She could have stayed home with her parents if she wanted to maintain this treatment. She chose to be with you and become your wife. Let her know she made the right decision. Hold her accountable, respect her as an adult, count on her as an adult, and most of all… love her. Adults make awesome mates…lovers… and friends.

In every adult relationship, there are rewards and consequences. When a husband allows his wife to be an adult, he tells her there are rewards and consequences to her actions. These rewards are more or less of him. When adults misuse the finances designed for the household, they may have fewer finances they are allowed to manage. When they begin to stay out late, the consequences may be less of the other they can receive. When they start to behave in a way that damages the relationship, they get to manage less of the relationship, such as the time spent together as a couple. Examples may be traveling to the same places in separate vehicles or not waiting for the other to assist; they will do it themselves or get others to help them.

The Over Apologetic Husband

Believe it or not, husbands make mistakes. Some are big, some are small, but they do make mistakes. Many add to this mistake by being over-apologetic, meaning apologizing for the same error repeatedly, every few minutes, days, weeks, or months. Understand this… when a mistake is made, it should be apologized for as soon as it is realized it is a mistake, even if it is not viewed as a mistake; if someone is hurt by it, apologize. Yet, if he continuously apologizes for that mistake, his wife may think the original apology wasn't genuine or sincere.

When a sincere apology is made, it should be given and done. There's no need to rehash what happened, meaning the person wronged shouldn't consistently hold the mistake over your head, thus leading to apologies number three… four… one hundred and thirty-four. Continuing to apologize may not allow you to heal and grow from the lesson learned. It can become a way to tear you down, a reminder of your errors, missteps, and failures. It is like having someone pick at a healing cut and watching it bleed again, only to say, "I told you it was not healed.".

Once an apology is given, it is no longer in control of the giver but now belongs to the receiver. They can either accept or reject it. Many men are constantly told their apologies are not sincere enough, and guess what? It never will be. Others hear their apologies are not heartfelt enough, nor will they ever be. They are told they didn't say it right or really meant it; they never will.

One primary reason these apologies may never be as the receiver requires is because DNA is different. There is no specific way to truly offer an apology. There is no particular tone, stance, language, look, or dress code for the apology. It is presented and expected to be moved on from; maybe still remembered but moved on from. Right? This is where the test of leadership comes in. Learning how to move on from a situation and not stay stuck in the same place discussing the same event in the same way in hopes that the response will change. What is it that they say about insanity? It's repeating the same actions repeatedly, expecting a different result. Not possible. The hardest part of the apology is learning to move on, learning from each other how to heal, and putting measures in place to prevent it from happening again.

When an apology is made, ask, "How can we move forward from this?" He should ask himself what can I do to help her heal, or how can I, as her husband, restore her trust in me? Ask her to be as specific as possible in her answers. This helps him to know where to start, where to focus, and how to get the family back on the right track. But it's not saying he will do these things. He should better understand what she needs, and hopefully, together, they will lead to a change in behavior.

Being Her Calm

Many things happen in a marriage that threatens the calm and peace of the house. They include finances, romance, friends, family, and even work. A husband must be the one who brings calm to any situation. He must be the one who looks at the case and brings peace to it through his words, actions, or sometimes both. Have you ever noticed in a relationship, job, sports, or anything, there is that one person who looks calm? It's not that he's not worried; he's just not letting the problem control him. He realizes the problem is solvable with clear, rational thinking and behavior rather than anger, frustration, and stress.

I am a big fan of Tony Dungy. Many years ago, when he coached the Tampa Bay Buccaneers and then the Indianapolis Colts football team, I would get frustrated watching him on the sidelines. The Colts would be losing, and he would always appear calm and relaxed. I'd yell at the TV, come on, man; get on your quarterback's case; chew him out; yell at him; at least look like you are concerned or care. He'd just walk the sidelines, talking into his headset and watching the game. Guess what? The Colts won the Super Bowl. He showed calmness has its place among chaotic situations and people.

When a husband constantly loses his calmness, he damages the marriage and the intimacy of the marriage. When taking a wife, I know some women tend to panic, stress, and worry, not that men don't (I had to put that in because I was afraid of being beaten up), but they do. Women tend to bring a lot of "what ifs" to the relationship, whereas husbands may consider will you instead. The question is, will he be her calm? She must be able to look to him, her husband, and calm down, realizing he has control of the situation. Her husband will solve the problem and protect her, no matter what. It's not that he doesn't worry or get frustrated; he just learns that God has him; He's got them both. God said, "I will never leave you or forsake you."

In Acts 27, the Apostle Paul demonstrates how to be Calm. Picture this.

There is a storm, and Paul is on board a sinking ship. What does he tell the crew? It will be ok. He tells them to eat to regain strength; not one life will be lost. How did he know? God told him. In the middle of the storm, he was more focused on the one who could calm the sea, say to the wind to be still, tell the waves to relax, rather than focus on the storm. Paul talked to God. Paul was much calmer that even the centurion responded differently in allowing the prisoners to live rather than kill them. Great leaders learn to present calm in the middle of the storm. Be the calm in her storm rather than the thunder and lightning in her life.

A husband must learn to say and mean, "We've got this; it's going to be ok. It will work out. Let's keep doing what we're doing; God's got it. We trust God, don't we? He must learn to admit when he doesn't know what to do but knows they've got it. He understands how to hold his wife and let her know it will be ok… relax babe. He learns not to return anger with anger, words with attack, and hate with hate. He learns to be the calm, her calm. As God is to him, he will be to her…her calm.

Boundaries

Every man should have boundaries set in place. These boundaries are designed to limit what he can and cannot do and what he will and will not allow in his life, job, friends, and family. Boundaries are needed for safety and protection, a better marriage, and a better life. If these boundaries are necessary for a man's life to keep him safe and prosperous, imagine how much more they are needed if he is married. A husband must have boundaries, especially with other women.

When a man becomes a husband, he must remind himself that not all his friendships benefit his marriage. He must put boundaries in place to ensure these relationships do not damage the one he has committed his life to, his wife. A husband must be able to set boundaries with his God, himself, his marriage, his kids, etc.

Boundaries should start simple and then, as needed…grow. For example, a husband should always tell his friends to "never put me in a position where I have to lie for you, and I won't put you in a position where you have to lie for me." So many boundaries are destroyed when men say and feel they must lie for their friends. They won't risk your credibility by putting you in an inappropriate situation if they are a real friend. You should be able to look in your friend's family's face, and they know you are telling the truth. Once you lie to your friends or ask them to lie for you, the cycle begins when they repeatedly ask you to do it.

Another boundary a husband should set is to always wear his wedding ring. This boundary lets other women and men know he is married and some things he will and will not do. It allows his wife to know he is not ashamed of his marriage; he enjoys her and doesn't mind letting the world know he is married and married to her. It also lets her know she can rest assured in knowing he is in it with her and not worried that he may feel he made a mistake in marrying her.

Setting a time to always try to be home is another boundary. This boundary keeps him as a husband out of unnecessary trouble in the streets and at home. What happens in the streets will affect the peace of the house. There is a particular time at night when trouble usually begins. Know that time and avoid it (usually around midnight). I knew a couple who would go out to a sports bar. They made it a point to leave the bar at midnight; no matter how good the game was, they would leave. When asked why, the husband replied that was when the danger would come in. This danger was other women dressing sexy more openly; some wanted to destroy what he had. That couple set boundaries.

A husband putting his wife's picture on his phone as a screen saver is another boundary that speaks that he is married, especially if she is wearing a wedding dress or the photo of them kissing, holding, or touching in love. Her picture shows everyone who sees it he is married; this is his wife, and he loves her. It also shows he values her and their marriage. Everyone worldwide recognizes the wedding dress and other poses or touches and knows what it stands for and represents ... love. Another boundary setting is putting her picture on his desk. Doing this sends a message to the office that this is his wife, and he loves her enough to show her off to the world. It declares to the world to leave him alone. He is married.

The phone is also a boundary; a husband should not keep certain things on his phone. Something that he knows will hurt his wife's feelings and possibly damage the relationship. Every husband should be able to leave his phone unattended and not concern himself with his wife using it or looking into it, not that this gives her permission to do so, but his boundaries are in place. He values himself and his marriage.

When boundaries are not set, anything and anyone can feel free to enter his marriage, and they will. They will enter and take things valuable to the marriage and its survival. They can jeopardize the peace in the marriage. Couples may argue about things that could and will destroy them individually and as a couple. Unnecessary items create more extensive arguments that last longer than necessary. When people feel content with invading his marriage, those invaders relish making him uncomfortable. They grow comfortable disrespecting him by calling him at all hours of the night. Imagine his phone ringing at 2 AM while he and his wife rest peacefully in bed. Not a good look, Sir.

When no boundaries are in place for the finances in the marriage, it stands to face challenges and, worst-case scenario, be destroyed. These finances are what the couple worked hard for, and if someone slowly drains them for their personal pleasure, they discount the needs of the household. As a couple, financial stability, advancement, and growth can lead to success. People will notice them for their success. They will begin looking for ways to join in without cost or risk. They will ask for purchases for themselves, loans, or materials that will benefit them and drain the marriage. When no boundaries exist, strangers, family members, and friends can come in and feel comfortable destroying his marriage. Set boundaries, now.

TESTED

Husbands will be tested in many ways; one way is to change the roles in the relationship. The husband becomes the follower, and the wife becomes the leader. It happens slowly, barely noticeable, and evolves quickly. In every organization, especially in a marriage, everyone has roles. Each role is as essential as each body part is. Husbands and wives must recognize this and cannot allow the enemy to convince either of them to change the leader's role. The roles of leadership align with God's divine order. The husband's role is leader, not a dictator, but a leader. The role of a wife is a helpmeet, not a servant or pawn but a helpmeet. In Genesis 2: 20 (NIV), There was no suitable helpmeet for Adam. God has a Chain of Command and holds each member responsible for their role; whether they are doing it or not, they will be held accountable.

Every house can have a male, but few homes have men in them. A man learns his role, does the work, and accepts responsibility, not by force but through God. A man is identified by his character, integrity, and honor. He is not perfect, but he does his best to be his best every day. He runs the race, fights the fight, and protects his family. There are days when he will want to run (we will cover this later), but God holds him still. There is a song that says, "He held me so I wouldn't let go." He learns to let God keep him.

There are examples of role changes in relationships. It could be when the wife is dictating the actions of the husband. She yells, scorns, or even belittles him; worst of all, some is done publicly. She dictates how the house is run, how finances are handled, and how the kids are raised. In some relationships, she controls what the husband says, does, and buys. The husband goes from the family leader to a laughingstock, even in front of his kids and family. He failed the test of standing firm, trusting his judgment, and, most of all, trusting God. Now, he fears being ridiculed by his wife. He covers up for this by saying, "You know how she is."

A husband must be aware and do his best not to fall for the role change. When God appointed man as the family's leader, He knew what He was doing. He really did. He made him to be solid and worthy of leading a great family. Look at a few examples of being tested. Remember Abraham and Sarah, how God told them of a child they would have, even in their old age, but it took too long. Sarah tested the relationship and came up with a new plan. She would take the lead, throw out God's plan, and implement her own. Sarah told Abraham her plan and his role in it. He offered no resistance; he just did what she said. It seemed like a great plan, right? Think about it. A wife tells her husband she has picked out this beautiful young woman for him to have sex with, and it is okay with her. No strings attached. Right! (He believed her). All that must happen is to get the woman, Hagar, pregnant. Many men would say okay. But the outcome resulted in unnecessary conflict, pain, and agony, which is still going on today. Guess who got the blame. Abraham.

Another example is with Adam and Eve. God put a plan in place, and Eve went with a new plan, hers. Eat or not to eat the fruit? Hmmm, she told her plan to Adam and convinced him to take part in it. It was a great plan, or so they thought. We can be like God! How quickly they learned the cost of being like God. It cost them everything. Compared to God's plan, their plan was flawed. Any plan not done in God's way is terrible. The great idea quickly turned bad, resulting in a punishment and eviction. God said You can't stay here anymore. You got to go.

When husbands allow God's role in a marriage to be changed, they fail the test. When he fails, all under the authority of that leader suffers, even down to the kids. But this failure does not mean destruction; it's not too late to regain the leadership role God appointed for the husband. The leader roles may have changed in the examples above, but they weren't changed with God. He continued to call and use the leaders to the roles He called them into. Nothing happened when Eve disobeyed God by eating the fruit. Even though Adam gave Eve leadership, their eyes were only opened when Adam disobeyed God and ate. Adam allowed his role to change, and the chain of command was circumvented. (I believe in my heart when Adam disobeyed God, the Holy Spirit was speaking to him, warning him not to do it, reminding him of what God directed). God communicates His plans for the family to the leader and confirms them through the helpmeet. God told Adam His intent and direction for the family. Adam's job was to inform Eve of God's plan. When a husband informs his wife of God's plans, he must ensure to tell her precisely what God said and how He shared it (Based on her faith, he may have to tell her after the assignment is done). This lets her know the seriousness of the plan AND God's intent.

God also uses this method to test and strengthen the leader's faith. God met Abraham where he was. He was intent on maintaining his faith and taking him to where He wanted him to be, from little faith to great faith, from stranger to FRIEND. His test was to leave his homeland and family with no clear direction on where he would go. Imagine a husband telling his wife, "We are moving, and I have no idea where we are moving to, but we're moving soon." That may go over poorly with the Mrs.... When she asks for an explanation, he tells her the God he has not known directed, he accepted, and we need to go. This was also a test for Sarah, his wife. Following God is simple but not easy. Knowing what must be done is simple. Doing it is difficult, especially when doubt creeps in. Abraham passed this test; he obeyed God and moved.

He was tested when God said to offer Isaac, his only son, up to Him as a sacrifice at a place where He would lead him, an area three days away. Imagine this test; should he tell his wife? What would she say? What would she do? Would she support or hinder him in this test? Had he told her, would she have tried to hold him back, and would she have been successful? Would she have traveled with him asking if he was sure God said to do this, begging him to ask God again? Would she have hugged her son while crying, consoling a bewildered Isaac who would now wonder what was happening? Would she have even cooked his last meal while crying over her son?

Notice how God handled the situation. He did not tell Abraham to tell or take Sarah with them. Abraham was the leader, so he chose to keep the information to himself until the test of faith was done. He knew what God told him to do, and he did it without even telling his wife or son; God responded, "For I know (experience) that you fear (honor, respect, believe, love) me, you have not withheld your only son from me." Sometimes, God will speak to a husband about things He may not want to share with his wife. The test is to listen to God… or listen to his wife.

In relationships, many women say there should be no secrets, even making promises never to keep secrets. Unfortunately, there will be secrets. Husbands will withhold information they believe their wives are not ready to handle or will mishandle it. This information will be something she knows is the correct thing to do, but she will only accept it with effort. However, God's plan must be first. This means some things will have to be sacrificed.

These things may be the wife's feelings or emotions. Imagine the emotions that flooded Sarah when she found out what her husband would do to their son… her only child. Imagine the joy she had knowing the blessings of an obedient husband to the mighty God (He did say He required obedience rather than sacrifice). Therefore, as a husband, it is knowing what to share and when and who to share it with. Everyone wants blessings from the test, but only a few want to go through the test. When God is obeyed, the people are blessed. He makes a way when there seems to not be one. I promise.

Galatians 6:9 (KJV): *Let us not become weary in doing good, for at the proper time we will reap a harvest if we do not give up.* This passage shows every test faced has a benefit, especially when obeyed and endured. These benefits are the reaction of others as they learn from the husband and wife how each behaved when tested. Isaac saw his father push, survive the test, and watched God show up and deliver on His promises. He witnessed his father prove he loved God more than the world. He mirrored his father's faith in God by establishing his own guide for his life. He trusted his father's wisdom to choose his bride, one whom he loved from their first meeting. He used it to live in a land that God determined and to look for a future kingdom as promised. He trusted God like his father did.

In marriage, every husband will be tested. The husband won't be worth much in battle without a test, especially a spiritual struggle. Every husband must be able to know and believe God can. Testing strengthens his faith when he takes the pressure off himself by placing it on God alone. As his faith grows, so does the way he lives his life. He changes from accepting wrong, sin, or abuse to living a life worthy of a child of God. A life of honor, integrity, and character in the sight of God. God gives second chances even more. Why? Because He loves and is love. He wants everyone to pass their tests of faith in Him. It is not His will that any should perish. He is very present, helping in times of need.

Another test is leading without force. A husband's role is not to make his wife obey or be submissive. The Bible does not say husbands make their wives submit, nor does it say to remind them over and over of their role in the relationship. This is God's job, and He's very good at it. He knows how to get the husband's and wife's attention. How? He works through the husband to get to the wife. The commands, not suggestions, of Ephesians 5 are designed to put the household in order. God is a God of good order and discipline (GOAD). When a wife refuses to be submissive to her husband (as unto the Lord), she disobeys Christ. A straightforward definition of submissive is if she will do it for Jesus Christ, she should do it for her husband. If Christ would ask either one (husband or wife) to do it, then it is not wrong. So… keep leading and walking forward with God. Husbands should allow God to change the way they look at their wives; she is His daughter, and He loves her very much. The way a husband treats his wife determines how his prayers are answered. Just a little note many men overlook: Ephesians 5 requires husbands and wives to be submissive to each other, but it does establish roles.

Another test is the anger and abuse test. This happens when you least expect and can spiral out of control. The Bible tells us it is okay to get angry, but in your anger, do not sin. A husband should never forget that his wife is his prized possession and an excellent thing. Remember, when a man finds a wife, he finds a good thing. She is not just a good thing; she is God's daughter, and He loves her very much. He does not like or condone his daughter's physical and verbal abuse. Plain and simple. A husband should not abuse his wife; hitting, cursing, or belittling, in any form, is not what God wants or condones. There is no excuse. There is no *"look what you made me do. No, it was just a little push, shove, or light hit; I barely touched you."*

Some barriers must be put in place to prevent abuse, not just put in place but adhered to. These barriers must be described, explained, and followed. Barriers such as when I raise my voice, let's call time out. Obstacles include name-calling, cursing, getting in each other's face, and yelling and screaming. Put a plan in place as quickly as possible to notice and prevent these things from exploding into verbal and physical assaults. Many women have said it was not the physical assaults that were bad, but the names they were called, which is challenging to get over and even harder to forgive. Those names echo in their minds, forcing them to wonder if that is what they are or how her husband sees her. Why would he say such things like that to her?

The husband is the leader, the man. He is the one the family looks to hold the standard. It is not easy, but it must be done. Walk away if he must. Go to a room and lock the door. Stand behind a table, at a desk, or in a car. Whatever it takes. Do something to limit the access to being violent. Situations, conversations, emotions, and other behaviors may push a husband to break. It may even be his wife who makes him, but his breaking point is not on her. She shouldn't be abused. Remember, she is a part of him. What he does to her, he does to himself. When he calls her names, he's saying this is who he married. When he hurts her, he's showing the world through her physical pain, the man he is, an abuser. "**HEY WORLD, LOOK AT ME, I ABUSE MY WIFE, THE WOMAN I LOVE, DON'T I LOOK _____** (fill in the blank)."

When he takes this action, the families come blazing into the marriage. She goes into defense mode with ready-made excuses: he's a good guy, or he just had a bad day. All the family knows and sees is that the husband has abused their loved one. Imagine what they think and, most of all, what they want to do to him in return. Things can get messy and grow messier than many ever imagined. Thus, put measures in place. Do it now. He should sit down and talk with his wife about these measures, what they are, how they will be implemented, what her role is in those measures, and what they should not be, but are. This protects the family, relationship, marriage, and intimacy. Do this quickly.

Rejection

A husband will face rejection, especially if he does what God has told him to do. A way to handle rejection is to avoid getting in the way. It's God they are rejecting, not him. In 1 Samuel 7, Israel wanted a king; Samuel, the prophet, was against this because he knew God was their King and tried to show them the error in their thinking. God told Samuel to listen to the people and everything they said. They have not rejected you, Samuel (so do not make this your problem). They have forsaken Me as their King.

What God did for Samuel, He will do for the husband: take him out of the line of fire. Tell him not to pick it up; it is not the husband's problem. A husband's leadership is defined by the way he follows Christ. It should not be taken personally when his wife does not follow him, as he follows Christ. It is not against him; it is against God. As the people did then, they do now. They reject God as their King, so a husband may be dismissed as the King's representative of his house. When this happens, there's no need to fight; remember, it is God's battle, not the husband. Continue to be a leader by following God.

When a husband is obedient to God and loves his wife, there are some disciplinary actions he may be told to take. These actions may not seem like love, but love has discipline. Love without discipline is considered abuse to the husband and to his wife. It may not be physical abuse, but it is abuse. When the husband does not implement discipline (not physical abuse) and guidance, the wife may feel she runs the relationship and is ready to handle the punishments given to the head of the house. She may begin to require all decisions to go through her. This may cause her to resent her husband more when all the stress of the relationship bears down on her. She will resent him for not being the leader she needs. This resentment will ruin intimacy.

Discipline should not come from anger, hate, or getting even but from doing what God says. As God told Samuel to tell the people the consequences of their actions, a husband should tell his wife the consequences of her actions. As Israel did with God, so it will be with the wife. She can accept or reject God's plan and His representative, the husband. This form of discipline may come in unanswered prayers, delayed blessings, sleepless nights, stress, frustration, and even anxiety. God may tell the husband what to buy and what not to buy, what to terminate and not terminate, even doing to her as He did with Pharoah, giving her over to herself.

Fear of Failure

Fear of failure is one of the biggest fears a husband will face. It triggers questions like, what happens if I fail? How will I look to my wife if I mess up? Will she believe in me? How can I tell her I failed again? Fear of failure may generate the attitude of refusing to try. It could cause fear of looking bad in front of her. With this fear, many husbands refuse to try anything they think they may not succeed at. This is damaging in so many ways. When fear of failure sets in, it takes root and grows. It affects all parts of the husband's life with the question, what if I fail? I read a quote that says, "Failures are a part of my life. If I don't fail, I will never learn. I won't grow."

Failure is "NOT TRYING; it's like not putting your name on a test. A husband enjoys looking good for his wife, being her superhero, and hearing her brag about him. He feels good about himself, but fear of failure causes him to pull back, withdraw, and hide, even from God (which we all know is impossible). He focuses more on himself than on God. This is an earthly thing with spiritual consequences. Slowly, he loses faith in God, the creator, putting more trust in men who criticize him. He forgets God's love and plan for his life and how He may prepare him for great things. This is part of the husband's training in making decisions. He is being prepared for what is to come.

When God looks for leaders in the church, His qualifications are on how the husband manages his family. He uses the family as a qualifier. He did not use a business, club, or organization. He did not say how he runs his business but manages his family. It doesn't mean that these things are not necessary. They are not the qualifiers. Leading the family requires all items to be seen, which can be hidden in other parts of life. The family sees it all. Learning to master this allows husbands to master things in all other areas. Learning to make decisions prepares the husband to run businesses, play a role in organizations, clubs, and sports, and be the leader of God's daughter. Great leaders recognize the family is most important and must be cared for and protected. They learn at home first before anyplace else.

Fear of failure causes visible damage to the husband in many areas. One area is in the family introduction. More women are introducing the family at events rather than the husband. In churches especially, many visiting families are presented by the woman rather than the man. The wife introduces the family, and the husband waits to be told what to do. This usually says he has a fear of failure, among other problems. He prefers to say nothing to keep from being wrong or looking bad, yet when he says nothing, it speaks volumes. It speaks of his decision-making abilities in the family. It also shows his doubts about decisions and possible fear of making them. It also shows these men are the ones who will say, "Let me check with my wife," more out of fear than out of respect. He does not want to be in trouble with her.

Another sign of fear of failure is a husband saying, "That's why I don't say anything; I don't feel like hearing about my mistakes all night." Husbands must know mistakes should be used as an educator, not an undertaker. It should be a teacher and encourager in his life. Working through the fear of failure makes the husband better and less afraid to speak. He steps forward and is not afraid to lead. God's plan for the leader is not failure. What others call loss, God calls success, a test, or even preparation for something greater.

The Bible speaks of Moses and Gideon, two men afraid of failure. Moses was content with feeding sheep in a foreign land. He tried once to be successful his way but failed, so why should he try again? Gideon was content hiding out, trying to separate the wheat from the chaff in his home so the enemy would not see him. Why be brave? It only gets you broke, or worse… killed. All God wanted was for them to trust Him. Notice God saw greatness when they saw failure.

Was Moses a success or failure? It depends on whether it is viewed from God's or man's eyes. It also depends on which side of the Red Sea an individual may be standing. Moses had a fear of failure. When God called him, he tried to convince God not to send him. He even complained of having speech issues. God was patient with him. He provided Moses with what he said he needed: a staff and his brother, Aaron, as a mouthpiece. What if Moses had not tried and walked away? What IF? What if fear had taken such a grip on him? He would not have seen God. I'm glad it did not happen that way. Moses went from nothing to something to nothing, then slowly back to something. But this time, it was done God's way. When he was running from Pharaoh in the wilderness, it looked like he failed. God's plan was done, or did it have to change? He lost his high-profile position with the most powerful man in the world, elite friends, and a heritage unlike any other. Yes, he lost it all because God had better plans. Moses learned the most essential part of decision-making: ask God first…trust Him above anything and everything you feel or think you know.

Fear of failure generates thoughts that are tricks of the enemy. They create burdens and stop the husband from trying. These thoughts cause husbands to question their value, worth, or capabilities to the family and God. Christ did not design, approve, or condone this. No husband is designed to question his worth to God or to anyone. Psalms 139:14 says, "I am fearfully and wonderfully created." "The enemy comes to steal, kill, and destroy (John 10:10). He says the enemy is a liar, the father of lies (John 8: 44)." He continues to lie to many husbands that they are a failure, makes too many mistakes and their wives no longer trust or believe in them. What lie has he told you? What are you doing about it?

This is a lot of pressure for a husband, especially a new husband. Imagine being more afraid of failing than enjoying success. Wanting to stop or refusing to try allows the enemy more control. It even causes disappointments.

Have you ever attended a youth baseball game and heard the parents yelling, "Throw the Ball"? The player, unsure what to do, just stands there, holding the ball and looking around. Runners take advantage of this opportunity to advance from base to base while the player with the ball is still standing there, not throwing it, afraid of making a mistake; yet, in the process, that player is making the biggest mistake by doing nothing.

Breaking news: Husbands are going to make mistakes. Let me say that again.

Husbands are going to make mistakes. Does making mistakes feel good?

Absolutely not! But it shows their vulnerability. It shows it's okay to be human. It also offers an excellent opportunity for God to show up and show out.

Many men speak of their fathers' taking chances, making decisions (good or bad), and learning from those decisions. They brag about their fathers' achieving success from mistakes. They learn by watching them make decisions like the men, fathers, and husbands they hope to become. Imagine a wife bragging about her husband not being afraid to make decisions. She can bring any issues to him and get guidance because she believes he knows how to fix any errors. He is not scared of failure.

2nd Timothy 1:7 says, "For God has not given us (you) a spirit of fear but of power, and love, and self-control (KJV)." Fear can control and restrict a husband from the promises of God. This doesn't mean husbands should rush boldly into any situation without consulting God. Remember, it says a sound mind recognizes danger and the guidance of God. A sound mind means just asking God what to do.

In 2 Samuel 5, King David sought the guidance of God. Should he go into battle and attack the Philistines? Read God's answer. Romans 8:28 says, "All things work together for good for those who love the Lord and are called according to His purpose." Making mistakes is not failure; it eliminates what doesn't work and allows God to show you what does. An old saying is, "I may not be able to tell you what works, but I can definitely tell you what doesn't." The path to success is eliminating wrongs and doing what's right. King David was mentally and emotionally beaten by his men. He had to encourage himself in the Lord. Husbands can do the same.

In marriage, many husbands fear the critique of failure, their mistakes, and how they will be reminded of it constantly. Sometimes, it is done so often that the husband decides not to make that mistake again. He will take no action, at least not in the house where leadership is needed. All authority is surrendered to the wife because of his fear of failure. Mistakes, not constant ones, happen, not to be torn down but to learn and build from. So don't give up, no matter what. A husband should use the same treatment on his wife. She will make mistakes. Don't hold them against her, but encourage her to keep trying. Let her know she is valuable and worthy to be your wife.

A few years ago, I was watching the Dallas Cowboys play. In the first quarter, the running back Emmitt Smith had about 12 yards rushing. At the end of the second quarter, he had about 30 yards rushing. By the end of the game, he had 150 yards rushing.

If he had given up in the first quarter (like the defense wanted him to), he would have missed the celebration at the end of the fourth. When mistakes are made, overcome them by not giving up. Look at the heroes of the Bible and fall in line with them. In Ecclesiastes, it tells us who wins the race; it is the one that endures to the end. Not the swiftest or the strongest, but the one who endures to the end.

Buy a Suit

This may seem like a strange thing to say, but every man, especially a husband, should not only own a suit, more than one, but should also know how to wear it. So many young men do not know how to wear a suit or tie a necktie. When a man takes a wife, he must be prepared for any occasion and ready to advance to the next level. His personal appearance is the first thing people see, especially when he walks in for a job interview. His appearance determines how he represents his family.

Believe it or not, a person's dress shows their desire to move up or remain the same. It shows their willingness to meet new friends in better circles, build better opportunities, or stay in the same cliques with the same friends. It shows if their relationship with their wife will grow to greater heights or stay right where they started. People who think they are on a dead-end road usually dress to match it.

As a husband, he should assess his marriage and his friend group. Are they the same friends he's had all along? Is his marriage prospering as it should, or are he and his wife just going around and around on the merry-go-round with the same friends, wanting nothing more than what they already have? A marriage should grow spiritually, mentally, financially, and physically (not getting fat). The leader must ensure this happens.

I have been on and conducted interviews with other men who, if hired for the positions they applied for, could have represented the companies better in how they dressed. They weren't wearing a suit. They applied for an important job and needed to care more to invest in their appearance. I could be wrong, but this position did not seem important enough for them to invest more in their future. Their mindset didn't represent the appearance of someone seeking. A husband must ask himself, "What does my family need me to do to be successful as a leader of our family?" Those who owned a suit looked as though it hurt to wear it; they did not know how to wear it, much less tie the necktie.

When a man takes a wife, he must understand how much she depends on him for the success of the marriage and the relationship. This may mean him leaving the mentality of some of his friends and gaining a new mentality of growing his marriage in all areas. As he takes this step, so does his bride. She realizes her dress may need to change to help the family be more successful. I have seen many women change their appearance and attitude once they noticed the dress of their man, but rarely have I seen men change their appearance and perspective based on the woman's dress. Thus, the man controls the direction.

The Argument

How did it start? Why did I say that? How did I let myself get pulled into this argument? It was so stupid. I was stupid. As a husband, I'm sure there has been a time when he has asked himself these questions or made these comments. The answer is simple. An invitation was given… and in all your machismo, challenge accepted. RSVP delivered with the time and date. As crazy as it sounds, it's what many husbands do. They willfully accept the invitation to arguments, never considering the trap being laid for them.

Imagine receiving an invite to an argument scheduled on a specific day and time. Should you accept? A husband will be baited and tempted many times. Yet how many of these… invitations will he keep getting? Couples constantly go at it but keep missing the point… what's driving these unpleasant meetings that go unresolved and open the door to each destroying the other with hurtful words or more. Frustration sets in, battle lines are drawn, and each opponent takes their appropriate corners. The man of the house, the leader, the husband begrudgingly accepts even when he has no desire to participate. He's in it now.

Arguing is a form of communication, something many couples say they don't do or do well. Arguing allows everyone to get their point across and let go of things they have been holding on to. The problem is that each may say things they should not have said or addressed when the issue initially arose. Think about it. It's not worth it: hurting their wife's feelings, apologizing, and making amends to prove a point? Really? Slinging dirt because the dirt was slung is what I call manning up. Manning up causes all sorts of trouble. Look at our prison system and hospitals. Ever noticed in an argument, within a few minutes, the original problem is no longer being addressed. Instead, it shifts to everything else, even cursing and name-calling. Arguing has resurrection power. It causes things that should have died long ago to come to life again. Imagine months of apologizing for a five or ten-minute argument because of a promise or refusal to acknowledge, right or wrong, something that tomorrow won't have the same value as it does today. Now he's agitated.

Arguing brings both parties close to playing in the enemy's ballpark and using their weapons. Imagine Christians using weapons designed to kill, steal, and destroy against one another. It causes one or both parties to defend themselves by deflecting what the argument is about. Then, bringing up something the other has done to hurt or shame them is irrelevant to the original argument. When this happens, it is a win-at-all-costs strategy. The question starts with, is what she is saying right? Is it true? Did I do or say that? All going unanswered or not given much thought. If it's true, why argue? Why try to better the odds of winning or making his wife feel unworthy? The husband should ask himself, have I ever done this with someone I love, choosing to prove my point to win, no matter the hurt or how long the pain takes to heal? Again, it is called manning up, winning at any expense.

Arguing is a willing action. No one can make the man argue. He, the husband, can choose to become a willing participant. It's a choice. He may decide to defend himself, causing him to forget that he can stop arguing by putting his lips close together, keeping them in this position, on pause for as long as it takes. I'm not saying there is anything wrong in defending himself. But... does it have to be in an argument? Can it be done in a conversation or even in silence? When an argument shifts to a discussion, listening takes place. When he listens to his wife's feelings, her emotions, frustrations, and hurt, this could lead to healing for them both. The attack stops, and he listens to his helpmeet, bride, and God's daughter. There are two critical words for turning an argument into a conversation. SHUT UP. Don't accept the invitation to the argument. Being quiet means one less person is arguing, one less person is frustrated, and one less person is using words of hurt and pain. Being quiet allows for listening without responding to take place.

Quietness shows a respect level that must be reached before responding. It's paying attention, acknowledging, and listening, but only responding once talking occurs. Being in this position is not identifying what will or will not be discussed. It's just being prepared to discuss anything for as long as it takes. It says this is how we will discuss and attack the problem... together. Neither party is being dominant, cocky, or egotistical. Both are working together to protect the marriage. The husband is watching the wife, and the wife is protecting the husband.

Another benefit to silence is not saying words of attack, damage, or malice. Words such as "you always; you never; or you are just like" show forgiveness has not occurred. They bring the future into the present by saying what will never happen, what a person will always be like or always have happened. Silence allows the husband time to talk to God and seek guidance and wisdom (James 1:5). Imagine what would have happened if prayer had been said during his last argument with his wife. Would the outcome be different?

In arguments, one person is rarely allowed to express their viewpoint. Words such as "Can I finish?" or "Will you just let me talk?" are often heard. As soon as something is said, the attack is on. Interruption takes place, and listening stops. The relationship is disrespected by one or both parties. Transparency stops, and sarcasm steps in. All the tools hell will allow are used or considered.

Some of these are: Yeah, whatever… sure you are… heard that before… really… stupid… dumb… idiot… and most of all… Fine (there are plenty more; these are just the basics). The verbal fight takes place. There's room for emotional, mental, and even physical damage using Satan's tools in a Christian life. Wonder how this process works?

Sometimes, arguments are used as a way of getting attention. "If you don't give me any attention, I will argue with you, create a commotion, and badger you; maybe that will get your attention." Some arguments show signs of hurt or loneliness. Some believe the other's response shows their level of love. But does this short-term attention-getter work, or does it lead to long-term frustration, confusion, or separation? I once heard about a wife who believed the more money she spent, the more attention she would get from her husband, good or bad. She captured his attention, but she also got a separation. Attention received outside of the will of God always leads to trouble.

A husband should always speak to his wife with love. Words are important and should be used carefully (because she gets on his nerves isn't a good reason to hurt her), at least not to God. A husband should not feel good tearing his wife down to prove a point. There is a severe problem with this. He is destroying a part of himself when he does it. It's the part that allows him to open his heart to receive and give love.

- What if his arguments sounded more like this:
- I know you're my pride and joy; however, I disagree with you.
- Sweetheart, you make a valid point; however, this is where my points differ.
- I may disagree with you, but I understand.

He should ask God to help him (husband) see the changes He is making in his wife rather than the changes he (husband) wants. God is always at work. He could be using the leader to show his helpmate grace, forgiveness, and more of Him as He used Christ to show more of Him. Where does that overflow go if God shows grace that overfills the husband's cup? On the floor or in the wife's saucer?

When Jesus was on the cross, He was attacked by those on the ground and the men on the cross next to Him. They called him names, spewed false accusations at Him, and even those who promised to stay with him…left. He had more than enough reason to doubt, hurt, and mumble. Yet, He only responded to those whose purpose was on God's will, doing what the Father wanted Him to do. He responded to John, His mother, and the thief who said, "Remember me when you come into your kingdom." He could have said and done much more, but… he didn't. As a husband, remember silence speaks louder than any words spoken in anger. Plus, it limits apologizing when nothing is said.

In many arguments, the mention of mothers comes up. It's your mother this or your mother that. How should this conversation be handled? There are a couple of ways to take this. Couples must be reminded that his parents are now her parents, and her parents are now his. Jesus also gave us a great example when the religious leaders talked about his mother. They insinuated she was a loose woman when they told him, "We know who our father is." Look how He handled it. He didn't respond. He kept silent and answered only to those things that mattered. His conversation was deliberate and only on what He chose to discuss. He did not allow the enemy to control the outcome. Hence, No Sin, No Apologies Needed.

Be Better Than You Were Yesterday

A husband's responsibility to his wife and family is to be better than he was yesterday. This means being physically, emotionally, spiritually, and mentally better. Get an education. A husband should always do his best to be prepared for his family's future. He can't do this by remaining the same man with the same education he had when he met his wife. Every husband should be prepared for the changing times which, are approaching faster than anyone can expect.

Continued education allows a husband to speak comfortably in many situations, whether at the PTA, his job, or community events. Many husbands fail their families because they have not furthered their education. Further education doesn't have to mean a college degree for those that school wasn't their thing. It could include learning from beyond where he was when he and his wife first met. He can elevate versus stay stagnant by learning to reconcile their income and expenses to their monthly bank statements, studying business fundamentals, or mastering marketing strategies. Education stagnation may cause stagnation in other areas of his life, especially finance. Intelligence and understanding are both needed. As the Bible says, a fool and his money will easily part.

Allowing himself to unlock his mind to learn more opens him up to being the first person his children turn to when they need help with their homework. It's not to say he must master everything, just have a better understanding, enough to be the one who can teach their children beyond what the schools provide. At a young age, they realize which of their parents has the intelligence to help them with what they need and which does not. An educated father and husband can use homework time to communicate and understand his kids. He will learn what they are going through and what they are weak in, increasing bonding time with his family. Suppose that man is not educated or does not better himself and advance his education. In that case, he may be excluded from the village, helping to educate his kids and redirecting them to other places for help like the teacher, neighbor, friend, or their mother. He'll miss great opportunities for teaching and bonding.

A better-educated husband opens doors for his wife to come to him with more problems she may face in her personal or professional life. He shows her he is better prepared to be a leader today than yesterday. He has walked through doors of all types of learning to better his family physically, emotionally, spiritually, and mentally. As a husband and father, learn to read better than you did before. Let your family see you reading. Let them see you grow in the home more than they see you grow outside.

A better-educated husband and father soon begins to change the way he speaks, the way he communicates, and the way he responds to others. The more you know, the more you grow. Get better, do better, be better.

The Yellow Sticky

I love yellow stickies. They can be used as reminders of things to do but are optional to stop what we are doing right now to do them. They remind us of what is and isn't important now. This is what should be done with some arguments or disagreements; they should be "Yellow Stickied." Have you ever been in a situation or environment, having a good time or at home relaxing, and an argument breaks out? If not, just wait…it will. This argument does not need to happen now. Can it be discussed later, and we just enjoy what we're doing now? I remember a story about a couple going on vacation. They argued the entire vacation about something that happened at the airport on their way to their vacation. When they landed, they barely spoke or acknowledged one another. They stayed apart as much as possible the entire vacation. This resulted in doing things separately. Their vacation was ruined by something they could have waited until they returned home. Could they have Yellow Stickied this situation?

When something is yellow stickied, the husband and wife agree by saying we are having too good of a time to allow it to be ruined with an argument or not spending time together. What's happening now is more important and should not be destroyed by an argument. We are more important than the incident. To implement, pick a time and date to discuss the situation. Doing this allows each to relax, prepare, revisit mentally, and get ready to discuss while objectively listening to each other's concerns. This is how a yellow sticky process should work.

Yellow Stickies can be discussed whenever both parties choose. The couple can appreciate the moment, create memories, and save money and time. They are not used as excuses to deny or hide from the situation but to keep from eliminating a disagreement or making a point of ruining the rest of the engagement. When the event is destroyed, many become upset because of wasted time and money. Feelings and thoughts arise from "We were having such a good time, then out of nowhere, we started arguing. Now everything is messed up." Sometimes, the Yellow Sticky works itself out before the time and date chosen to discuss it. One or both may consider the other's point of view and admit an error was made in judgment, or the issue is not as vital as it initially seemed. Either way, both enter the Yellow Sticky conversation clear-headed (hopefully), calm, and with their defenses down, especially if the event was enjoyable.

In John 10:10. Jesus says the thief comes to steal, kill, and destroy. This means the enemy wants to destroy whatever good time was in God's eyes. Yellow Stickies are not used to show your wife she's important, that her feelings and opinions matter. She should already know her value to you and shouldn't doubt them, nor should they come into question during the yellow stickied conversation. If they do, he may have more issues than he realizes. When a time and date is set, do it. The husband and wife must agree to the change if it gets pushed back. Yellow Stickies allow the couple to grow stronger individually and together.

Many couples only move forward once they solve the issue. This can slowly destroy their relationship because the subject can keep them stuck in the same place trying to resolve an old problem that, nine out of ten times, neither remembers what or why it was an issue in the first place. I was told sixty percent of relationship problems go unsolved; they have no solution. Many couples need to be stronger to handle the issues because the answers they want aren't what they get. They want God to tell them one thing, and He tells them something else.

Sometimes, we must move forward to get stronger and go back to resolve the situation. Getting stronger means building more trust in God, yourself, and one another. He, the husband, may begin to see things from his wife's perspective and hopefully understand there may not have been an attack. She may just have been showing her emotions through hurt. When they are stronger, the situation looks lighter and achievable.

When a conversation is Yellow Stickied… honor it or fight about it later. The choice is obvious. I suggest that the husband buy some stickies for his car and home, or if he's more techy, download an app and have them ready.

Go Stand in the Corner

Sometimes, I ask the husband and wife a two-fold question in my counseling sessions. The question is like a double-edged sword. Her answers and reactions will say a lot about the relationship and her. This is the question, "If your husband walks into the room and tells you to stand in the corner, what do you do?" You can imagine some of the reactions I received. The calmest women suddenly change. There may be some neck rolling, eyes stretched wide, body tensing, and smirks. I observed the changes in their expressions and suspected some unkind words might spewed in my direction. I'm usually surprised when I hear no from Christian wives, followed by "He needs to explain why I am going in the corner." Then I share the rest of the question, "What if there is danger in the house and he does not have time to explain to you the danger? If he knows you are in the corner, he can direct the attack to the enemy to protect you and your family. If you are arguing, both of you are in danger."

In many areas around the world, they have an emergency warning system. This system lets people know there is imminent danger and that they should reach a safe space. It does not mean stop and ask why, where, or how. Those who stop to ask these questions put themselves and others in danger. Imagine hearing an alarm and not responding to it. How many people are hurt, especially first responders, because people ignore the warnings and must be saved, rescued, or protected? It's incredible how many people think they know better and choose not to take heed of the signs, those blaring lights and alarms. Their choices put the first responders in danger by turning the responders' focus away from others who may genuinely need help to rescue the reckless.

The wife's answer not only speaks to the character but also speaks to her connections to her husband. Stay with me. The wife may seem unwilling to relinquish her independence and fully trust her husband. Is she fighting for her rights as a woman where no one will tell her what to do, especially a man? Is she feeling she's equal to any man, especially her husband? It may also speak of her inability to trust men. Will she double-check everything her husband tells her or suggests she do?

For the husband, it speaks to his integrity and character. These may be in question if the wife finds him untrustworthy. Why? Has he abused his words so often that she no longer believes him? How many times has he failed or disappointed her ON PURPOSE? Does this sound familiar? Does his wife still believe what he says, and most of all, does he keep his word as much as possible?

One of the main words in Ephesians chapter 5 is submissive. It not only applies to the wife but also applies to the husband. It applies to Christ, for He submitted to the will of His Father, who created a body for Him to live in. He offered Himself to the point of death, actual death, making sure all He did was honor His Father.

As a husband, honor your wife with words and actions, from things done when she is near and when she is not. These things may not be necessarily right or wrong, good or bad, but are done in honor of her. It may involve who you speak to and how you speak to them. Does this bring honor to her, things that you look at, buy or even withhold? How will people see in her by looking at you?

Earlier, we discussed integrity. A loss of integrity can hurt the husband and his family. How hurt would he feel knowing his family viewed him as a liar and they moved or didn't move to safety? If the husband is habitually late, full of excuses, or a showoff, he degrades his family's trust in him. When it comes to bills, is he consistently paying them late? Has his wife lost faith in him and is worried about repossessions, cut-off notices, or worse... eviction? Does she start making provisions for herself and the family? DANGER AHEAD! She may no longer trust her husband as much as she could...or should.

Would you believe some wives are more surprised when their husbands do right than when he does wrong? I spoke with a wife once who said her husband went to the store and came right back. Usually, it would take him hours, but he did it in minutes this time. She was surprised. Doing something right shouldn't be a surprise to his wife. He should be able to tell her to stand in the corner, and she should (not say she will) because she knows he's not trying to make her look foolish, show off, flex, or test his manhood. As a husband, be trustworthy. A fire alarm that keeps going off when there is no fire will not be trusted. It will be ignored, and the family could get hurt or killed.

Destroying trust doesn't happen instantaneously. It begins at some point, then continues to grow... and grow...and grow. Husbands can look back and see where it happened and how. It may have started with forgotten appointments, secrets, friends, habits, attitude, work, money, being consistently late, not helping around the house or with the kids, just to name a few. This is where his wife may no longer feel honored as his wife and helpmate. Even lousy spending habits or hiding funds for the wrong motive can destroy emotion and cause mistrust. Most of all, not carrying your share of the load in the house (whatever you two decide) can be damaging. The husband should ask his wife why she may be losing his trust and work on fixing this. He shouldn't get his guard up or get into feelings because he doesn't like what she says. This response is not a personal attack but an honest answer meant for the betterment of the family. The two should put a plan in place as quickly as possible. Nothing changes overnight, but there is no better time to start than with one another.

In Genesis 18, Abraham runs to his wife Sarah and tells her to quickly cook a meal for three strangers. The Bible didn't mention Sarah arguing, complaining, or even getting upset. She didn't tell Abraham his friends must go home, his friends need to bring their own food, or his friends don't pay bills in this house, she is not his maid, or she's too tired, go get Hagar to do it. Sarah prepares Abraham's meal as he's requested. In doing so, she's preparing a meal for God (yes, God in the flesh), and He eats it. Abraham had done a lot in the past for Sarah to say he was not trustworthy and compromised his integrity, yet she remained obedient. Why? Because Abraham got better. His consistent efforts in being trusted with the small things proved he could be trusted with the more significant things. His wife got up and prepared a meal for God. Through his integrity and honor, his wife was blessed with a gift she longed for. She received news that against all odds, nature, and time, she would give birth to a son, one she'd yearned for so long.

The husband's behavior sets the tone for the family. The personality of the leader is exhibited in the people. Trust God and know His word matters no matter what people say or do. If the husband wants his wife to stand in the corner, he, too, must be willing to stand in the corner as if Christ were to tell him to do so. He will say to the husband to forgive, love, and pray. God has proven Himself trustworthy. Don't believe it? Check his resume.

T.R.A.P

Social media is filled with so many frustrations. Many of these are half-truths and are full of lies, especially regarding relationships. There are pictures of couples cuddling, those of women sleeping on their men, adorned with quotes of love (what it is, what it looks like, and what it should be). Rarely does it match the scripture. There are couples in great shape cooking or even working out together. There are posts of times spent together, and even places traveled. Look closer at the captions or snapshots. You may fall into the T.R.A.P. (Thinking Relationships Are Perfect).

When you fall into the T.R.A.P., you begin questioning your relationship and what you're doing wrong. Why doesn't our relationship look like theirs? I wonder who took the picture. Did they pose for this while someone was walking around with a camera? Is it staged? If we're not careful, this T.R.A.P. way of thinking can lead us to believe we must be doing something wrong because they appear so happy and in love. They look like they will give or do anything to be together. Notice all the beauty and little flaws of the woman in the picture. A man may begin to think that he wants a woman just like that one. They appear to have no problems, and she really loves her man.

I discovered or realized that they only show you part of the account. They only offer a glimpse into their story. In other words, part of the truth is a whole lie. These snapshots, or T.R.A.P.S., may not show hurt, pain, struggles, anger, frustration, deceit, or abuse.

They only show couples looking hopelessly in love and in perfect harmony. But why? Many people post pictures to prove they can overcome bad times, hurt, or pain, hoping these pictures will tell the world how much they love each other. How do you feel when you look at these pictures?

The enemy wants us to believe we are failing in our relationships and God's way isn't working. Why not try it our way? Everyone has difficulties in relationships. Unless you understand this, you'll do relationships the devil's way, which is in any other way than God's words. The book of James says when, not if, but when we face temptations, trials, and tribulations, we will face difficulties for our faith and our marriages. Many say, "See, that's why I won't marry," or "That is why I am alone." I respect these opinions, but I fear they miss some great times. Remember, God said, "It is not good for man to be alone." People who feel this way about marriage are called lonely. When we quit caring about people, we close off one crucial thing about God: He is a God of Relationships. He said it is not suitable for man to be alone.

When a man enters a relationship, he must consider Romans 3 23: All have sinned and come short of the Glory of God. He and his partner are two imperfect people coming together as one. This requires significant adjustments for them both. Problems occur when we expect each other to suddenly become perfect but not require perfection from ourselves. Two imperfect people, having flaws, issues, and so many other things, willingly join in unity forever. This is the difficulty many need to realize. When we fall into the TRAP, we must remember we will have problems. Our wives are not perfect, and neither are we. We will make mistakes more than once and have some difficult days together.

Perfect relationships consist of people with scars from time and mistakes growing together, hanging on to each other and God. An ideal relationship is a man knowing his wife has a way of showing she loves him. He must know that way, accept it, and move on. One gentleman told me he knew his wife loved him because she would buy him his favorite snacks when shopping. That was her way of showing love. Another said he knew his wife loved him because she would do his hobbies with him. One guy said his wife would touch him on his shoulders as she passed by. These men learned to recognize the signs of love and accept it. The actions mentioned above are what their wives did for them, but what would you do? Have you ever said, "Even if she does nothing, I will give all I have to God first and her next daily?" The perfection we demand must be the perfection we are willing to give. If we cannot offer perfection, quit demanding it. We are falling into the TRAP.

Thinking relationships are perfect is as crazy as believing Christians are perfect. Things are only sometimes what they appear. Relationships become great when they can understand and deal with their problems and not allow their problems to separate them, no matter what. These couples protect their weak areas by not telling the enemy their weaknesses. How do you say to the enemy your shortcomings? By letting him know when we'll quit. Think about it. What is it we won't tolerate? What are our relationship killers? What will make us stop and walk away? When we can answer these questions, there is an excellent possibility what we just said will happen or worse. We become so busy defending those areas that the enemy will sneak another way. When we inform the enemy of our weaknesses, he will use them against us. If we were fighting Superman, what would we use as a weapon? Kryptonite, right? Why? Because he said, that is his weakness. Why would we use anything else?

Like Superman, we are delusional when we tell the enemy our quitting points and expect him not to use them against us. Why tell him our weaknesses and not our strengths? Tell him the foundation of our faith, our hopes, and where our joy is centered. Tell him what the cross did for us. Tell him what God has promised us. Many of our parents and grandparents are celebrating double-digit anniversaries. Why is that? Could it be they weighed and continued to weigh the cost of their relationship and looked for ways to strengthen it rather than destroy it? The best step in relationship building is to ask God to help us look at ourselves before we look at our wives (you know that scripture, that log in your eye before the speck in hers).

I've met couples who told me their deal breakers; whatever that deal breaker was, it happened. Could we take our wedding vows lightly, or maybe we forget them? Remember that part that says, "For better or worse, sickness and in health till death do us part?" When we tell ourselves this marriage is killing me, is lame, and is not an excuse to leave. Try again.

I believe every marriage should have the vows pasted in the house to remind them of their commitment to one another and God. He took them seriously, very seriously. We should stop looking at other relationships and gauging ours against theirs. Focus on ways to become a better husband for God so our wives can enjoy a better man every day.

Do our part and watch God do His.

The Blind Side

The blind side is when one person in the relationship tries to catch the other off guard to win or prove a point. They're blindsided. Never saw it coming. Their partner is prepared, guns loaded and waiting for them to move into the designated area, and before they know it, they swoop in for the attack, just like a serpent or roaring lion. This behavior displays a lack of respect for the relationship, which means a lack of respect for the husband and the wife.

Husbands must love their wives and respect them. It's not optional. God has commanded it as such. Unfortunately, many fall short because of ignorance in doing the necessary things for husbands to love their wives. The blind side is designed to catch the other off guard, unprepared, to tear them apart. Blind siders demand their wants on their terms, in their time and space, but won't connect emotionally, at least not in battle. They want the other person, their opponent, defenseless, not only to win but to destroy them, thus causing further damage to the relationship. Sometimes, being a Christian but using the enemy's tools is not a good look. Blind siders forget that these tools can steal their joy, kill the mood, and destroy the passion in the relationship. It may even damage the person physically, mentally, and emotionally.

The Blindsider usually begins with "We need to talk," generating alarm bells, doubt, and thoughts of "What did I do now?" The only time I hear this is when I have done something wrong, not when I do something right." When these words are said, self-preservation kicks in, and the focus is no longer on the problem but on protecting myself from whatever is coming. The conversation tends to go downhill, and everything still needs to be resolved. So... when his wife walks in...she hits him with, "We need to talk." How does he respond? How does he maintain integrity, respect, honor, and character to stay focused on the problem presented?

Using this becomes an opportunity to attack the person, not the problem, nor does it usually end with a solution. When the problem is presented in this manner, battle lines are drawn, and defenses come up. Don't get all sanctimonious with me now (We all do it), which may cause our partners to shut down and become unwilling to discuss anything further. Words like "I don't know, I don't have time to talk about that right now, or I am too tired to discuss this mess; I've had a hard day." are off-putting and may not sit well with us. "If what we're doing is not working, why are we still doing it?"

A better way to do this is to allow the other person, husband or wife, the same time to tackle the problem. It allows the couple time to maintain respect for one another and for their relationship. If either has been contemplating a problem all day, give the other all day to do the same. This respect shows they care more about one another and less about the issue. It's not that the problem isn't essential, but their love for one another is more important. They respect each other and, most of all… their relationship.

When the Blind Sider loses trust in God, they try to take control of the situation to achieve victory. But the victory is not as sweet as they would like, and someone gets hurt. The goal of not being a pushover has been accomplished. The Blind Sider goes from a wimp to someone who pushes others away, pushing away the one they love most. Communication breaks down. Who wants to share with someone who tears them down?

The Blind Sider has another destructive effect on communication. The receiver fears what is being said will be held against the other later and used in an argument. Blindsiding damages intimacy. It damages holding, touching, laughing, or even sharing. It causes the atmosphere in the home to change. The husband or wife may sit in the car longer than needed once they get home, wondering what the mood is on the other side of the door. Rather than feeling happy, they feel anxious. They are home and should feel relaxed. Couples withdraw from one another, each playing their roles, with limited communication, for fear of an argument or disagreement. Again, intimacy is damaged, time together is damaged, and more time apart is becoming routine.

The damage to intimacy is done and takes longer and longer to repair. Driving together becomes worse and worse. The radio does all the work, and both half-heartedly listen to the music. One may think about what to say or what not to say to avoid getting in trouble while the other focuses on all the other person did wrong and how this relationship cannot go on this way. He must change.

Couples complain they do not talk, but they fail to realize how they've damaged the security of the other; there's no safety in the presence of the other. They've attacked each other until the house is no longer a home but a prison that each desperately wants to escape. Each day, it becomes easier to leave and harder to return. And for what? To win arguments or to prove points. Congratulations! You've won and lost at the same time.

Blindsiding is the worst thing a husband can do to his wife because he represents Jesus. Is this the light he wants to show Jesus in? Is this how his wife is supposed to see him? Is this what he wants to be as her husband? Most of all, is this what Jesus shows when He is seen? When someone is blindsided, it shows them they are unsafe in the other's presence. It shows them that the answer to the question is more important than anything… including them. There must be an answer NOW.

People say, "Just tell me the truth," but they show so much hostility that proving **The truth** is not accepted unless it lines up with what they believe is true. Ask yourself. Can your wife feel comfortable telling you the truth? Is the answer more important to me than her? Are you willing to damage intimacy for an answer?

A wife should always feel safe in her husband's presence; she should be able to tell him anything. Not that it will be agreed with, but she will not be physically, emotionally, or mentally attacked. She won't be belittled because of a disagreement. Blind siders feel they must always win. They call or show up to the other's job, activities, hobbies, and events just to say, "Baby, I support you." Really? But why? What do they expect to accomplish? If a person is destroyed, the change is not what anyone likes. The outside will not match the inside, and an explosion is bound to happen. If a husband knows his wife is not being honest, he should confront her, if confronting her is going to help. How should he confront her? How will he restore her?

The Apostle Paul wrote about restoring a brother or sister, not damaging them because they got caught. True confession changes the heart of a person.

Actual attacks change the method and motives, not the person.

Listening Rather than Solving

Being a husband means listening. Yes... lots, and LOTS... of listening, not necessarily responding to everything, just listening. It lets her know she is appreciated for her mind and body. This allows her to know she matters, both at work and at home. It helps her overcome the negative influences of social media, family, and friends.

There is a video of a husband and wife talking on a sofa. She shares her pain, and he tells her what it is and how to solve it. They go back and forth in the discussion, each becoming more frustrated. The frustration is because men are problem solvers; they see or hear of a problem and take the direct route to solve it. Sometimes, they have great results, but they act. Some men are like Tim the Tool Man on the TV show Tool Time; whereas they know how to do it, but the results are usually painful, expensive, or both. Men are problem solvers, which is what men do... solve problems. Many men are mission-driven and sensitive to time.

I remember driving cross country with my family. The map said how long it should take to get there, and I was determined to beat that time. Guess what? We did it in less time, and I was ecstatic. I'd accomplished the mission by only stopping for gas, food, or essential rest. Still, I missed opportunities to listen and enjoy the family.

In the video, the wife is upset because she wants her husband to hear her, pay attention to what she's saying, and not try to solve the problem. She wants to be heard, noticed, respected, and acknowledged for her thoughts, primarily when she works with people who may have disrespected, belittled, or stressed her out. The wife mentally has a throbbing headache, and the husband sees the problem and tries to give her the solution to stop the pain instantly. The pain was not as significant as her being heard and appreciated by her husband.

Therefore, wives want to be heard by their husbands, not judged. They want to talk to them and know they are listening rather than attempting to solve their problems (yet). Even though the husband may know what to do, learn the difference when she shares or asks you to solve her issue. Remove all distractions as much as possible, and give her your undivided attention. Show her what she has to say is more important than what is being done at the time. Pray she does not make this an all-day affair and understands that a sporting event isn't the best time to get your attention.

What are the benefits of a husband listening to his wife? An old saying is, "With whom you share your emotions with, you will share your bed with." Is that benefit enough? She needs to feel emotionally connected to her husband in all things. Wives share their emotions, feelings, and hearts with their husbands. Many wives who have strayed when asked why they said, "He understood me. He listened to me. I felt he cared for me. He showed love when I needed it." When a wife knows her husband is listening to her, she pours out her heart. This pouring out makes her more emotionally attached to her husband as a friend and lover. When a wife is pouring out her problems, as a husband, do not attempt to solve them for her or tell her how to feel. Just listen and make sure she is aware that you are… listening. If she doesn't ask, don't offer suggestions. The book of James says to be slow to talk and quick to listen. Maybe, therefore, God gave us two ears and one tongue to listen more and speak less. It's great when a wife can't wait to get home to talk to her husband about her issues; when she feels her husband is connected and understands her, she appreciates his efforts. To achieve this, a husband should prepare himself daily for the pouring out to his wife. It is well worth it.

Being married is not easy (then again, neither is being single); both take work. Some days, it will feel like the husband gives more than he receives. Imagine how God feels. He gave more than anyone ever will. The Father, gave us His all. He gave himself. If He can, then so can we, with His help. The more a wife opens herself up emotionally to her husband, the more chances he must be her hero, a title many husbands will relish. He may imagine hearing her say, "My husband is all the man I desire."

The benefits of a husband's emotional sharing with his wife lead to great intimacy. She doesn't have to fight her emotions to be with him (this happens more than most men will ever know). She feels fantastic being herself around him and comfortable being in intimacy with him, falling deeper in love with him; I hope and pray this is what husbands desire. God Bless!

Understanding Your Wife

Understanding your wife is not simple, no matter how it is put, it's not. She will try to get her feelings, thoughts, hurts, and emotions understood. Many wives say their husbands don't understand these things, and they don't because the DNA is different. A husband shows and responds to love differently. Most husbands will offer the action part of love, while most wives are looking for the emotional with action part of love.

An excellent example of this is the way gifts are given. Women give gifts with a bag, cute paper balled up and stuff in the bag, ribbon, and even a pretty card. When men give gifts, it is different; she is lucky if he takes time to wrap it and get a card, especially the card.

Many husbands understand the definition of love but need to know how it applies to their wives. Does she view love as holding, touching, warmth, a smile, whispers of sweet nothing in her ear, safety, and protection? Many husbands may apply love as respect, wives cooking for them, and sex (definitely... the sex) and not recognize his wife needs love applied her way to initiate intimacy and sex. Husbands need sex to initiate love. Same word, different application.

Every husband should ask his wife how she wants to be appreciated. How does she like to be shown love? How can he do a better job showing her love? He is not saying he will do these things, but now he better understands what it is, and it may change how he looks at her. When a husband asks these questions, he should accept clear responses that lead to understanding. Husbands ask their wives to be as specific as possible. Don't rush her; allow her the time she needs to answer.

A husband should not remind his wife, of all he does for her, how he works a job he probably doesn't like, with people he doesn't like, and things he buys her. It is not a good way to show love. She already sees these things; she may just want him to learn her views and how to apply them to her. He should listen and use what he knows about her to her and for her. He knows more than he thinks. He should not be manipulated into pleasing her or go against what God has said. An old saying goes like this: "If you love me, you will," This should not be used to get anyone to do something against what their core is telling them is inappropriate or is not the right time. Nor should it be used in a negative way to get needs met. Husbands must be better than that. They are God's representatives.

Understanding wives means understanding love as much as possible and realizing it involves appreciation. Show her she's appreciated. Say Thank You. No matter how large or small, just say Thank You. This is being a better husband for God by learning to love His daughter better. Everything a husband does should be for God, but his wife receives the benefits or lack thereof. Lack of appreciation hurts both the husband and his wife. Showing appreciation draws them closer by shaving off small edges of roughness and allowing each to be a little tender to the other. Sometimes, a husband may feel his wife could show more appreciation. This usually generates questions like why try, she won't notice. If a husband holds his wife to an appreciation standard, he should ask himself, does Christ hold him to the same appreciation standard, and can those standards be met?

To better understand his wife, a husband should ask God to help him. 1 Corinthians 13 says, "Love keeps no record of wrongdoings." This might be an excellent time to eliminate any evidence proving a point against her.

Today, many men feel like they must be hard. There are better ways of understanding wives, which could lead to showing love the wrong way, cold and callous. The strong, tough guy works in the movies but could cause loneliness in real life. As a husband, he should take time to learn, relax, and enjoy the wife God has given him and embrace how God is allowing him to better their relationship and marriage.

Pay Yourself

Many years ago, as a young lad living at home with my parents, I remember going to them and asking them for money to buy this or that. Then, I got a job and began making my own money. Talk about a significant ego boost. I remember the first hard-working job I had. I worked so hard for my first paycheck. I was proud. It took me a week to cash it. I kept staring at it and thinking, "I earned this check."

One mistake husband makes is handing all their money to their wives to pay the bills. This is a mistake because now he must go to his wife for money, his money, the money he worked for. Then it turns to why he needs money and what happened to the money she gave him last week.

Everyone who works should get paid for their work, plain and simple. A husband who must ask his wife for money may make him feel like he's less a man and more her child. Why? Because it may take him back to when he was a child and had to ask his parents for money. This may cause him to feel as if he hasn't grown up because now, instead of being accountable for his money, he must ask for it again from someone else: his wife. He will begin to rebel because he feels controlled; it will become tiring unless something changes. He will start to hide money, get an attitude at anything his wife says, and begin using words like she's trying to control me or nobody owns me.

Some people have issues handling money and may require support and assistance. I'm not saying that this is a bad thing. We all need help. If not now… soon. Finances are significant in a man's life. The Bible tells us God placed Adam in the garden to work the garden. A man was designed to work and intended to get paid for his work. Some wives use money to control or to keep their husbands in check. They may not realize that doing so hinders them from becoming the men they want to be and stunting their ability to develop. It reduces him a bit every time he must ask his wife for money.

Some men may say, "Let me ask my wife for some money to get this?" What a way to hit the pride and ego. Our pride and ego make us (good or bad) …they make us.

When a man begins working, something in him changes; call it improved self-worth or a better self-value; either way, he feels good about himself. When he pays for himself, he gets a better feeling of self-worth. He holds his head slightly higher, stands taller, and confidently walks. Paying himself means he's paid for his efforts. He and his wife should determine his amount, but… he must pay himself. He deserves to pay himself!!

Financial planning also plays a part in his role as a husband and how well he plans for his family's future. This usually is not an easy subject, so he should still do it no matter how he approaches it. A husband should sit down with God and find out what role He has for him and his family, then plan for that role and that goal. Genesis 37-50 tells Joseph's story and rise to power. He went from the jailhouse to the White House, or in other words, to the castle. At one point in Joseph's life, he became Pharaoh's financial advisor. In his plenty, he should prepare for his famine. When he has a lot, he prepares for when his lean times will come, as he knew they would. Joseph told Pharaoh to save because they would have seven years of plenty, then seven years of famine. In their preparation, they made it a little hard on the people. The tightening of Joseph's budget caused the people some discomfort, even causing some to complain. The husband's family may do the same, yet look at the result. They had all the necessities they needed.

Husbands learn from mistakes, those made by them or by others. Look at things recently purchased, needed, or would like to buy. When considering a purchase, he should ask himself if it is something he needs or wants. Could he purchase something with cash, or will he need to use other people's money, like credit cards and loans, to pay for them? Many men say, "Knowing what I know now, I would not have gotten them, or I would have saved much more money to lower the payments." Look at the long-term cost of an object. If funds get tight, can the family still make the payments? If sickness happens, job loss, job changes, or his wife gets pregnant, will they still be in good shape financially?

This means husbands will teach their families to set aside funds for that day of famine. The more they set aside, the better they can go through famine. This includes paying off as many bills as possible, monitoring their income-to-debt ratio regularly, and ensuring it looks good. He's teaching his kids the responsibility and benefits of being financially wise.

In financial planning, he and his family should have financial meetings at least twice a month. These meetings should involve everyone in the household. The sessions will teach kids the family budget, credit score, credit cards, bank statements, writing checks, and saving. It shows them what comes in and what goes out. Teaching them money's value and handling it is a crucial lesson in their financial success. Wisdom allows the family to retire when God wants and enjoy life with the least stress possible. The family will appreciate this very much.

The Blended Family

As mentioned earlier, taking on a wife is very serious. When a man takes a wife, he is taking all she has. He is taking her family as his family. He is taking her bills as his, and her kids are now his. Yes, her kids are now his kids. Let that sink in.

He can't choose which of her kids he claims, nor can she do that with his. Her kids all come with her. If he leaves one out, he will risk leaving out a part of her, a part of her life. That part, that piece of her heart that's been left out, may be what holds the rest together.

Blending a family is just that, blending. The family is integrated, so telling them apart in love is complicated. When the I dos are said, the family is now blended. The quicker this is understood and accepted, the deeper the blending can begin. "her kids and my kids" should not be used again. All the children must know they belong to the family and are "our kids." The first step begins with the husband showing love and not using it as an opportunity to implement discipline, get those kids straight, or set things in order.

He may feel the kids need to be taught respect and manners, but how does it look from their side? Do they think he needs to be taught love and compassion? Before implementing discipline, show love. Every family must have love, and it should start with the husband. The Bible says God is love. A husband must do his best to reveal who he is through God's love.

Let them know he will do his best to love them unconditionally, and he will need help being loved unconditionally as well. Be honest and admit that he will make mistakes but improve over time through those lessons and errors. Most importantly, he will make himself vulnerable to love and be loved. Teach and show the entire family how to hug, hold, laugh, and, yes, even shed some tears.

His wife will stand in awe to see how he has blended the family. This type of love eases tension and pressure from his wife. Bringing a new man into her children's lives is a worry most wives have from the first date. She worries about becoming the go-between with her husband and the kids. She contemplates taking sides and being accused of showing favoritism for him, his kids, or hers. She frets over how the kids will get treated in the family. Will he be stricter or leaner on her kids? Will he even care? Will they be too much for him to handle and the relationship? How will the kids get along? Put her mind at ease. Let her know that will not be the case with this family.

In a way, God has a blended family. Romans 1:16, God's family now consists of Jews and Gentiles. Knowing which of these families He's a part of doesn't matter. He loves us so much. The husband should follow this example and love them all the same so no one can tell the difference.

The leader of a blended family will face times when discipline is necessary. It should be done with love, even demanding a hug after the discipline. Always get a hug. This shows love. A love strong enough to correct them and hold them to a standard set for the family. This hug is part of showing grace, God's grace.

There may come a time when one or both parents, either in the marriage or exes outside the marriage, may say they don't want the new father or mother to discipline their child. Each spouse may handle this in one of several ways. One way is to let the other parent (the ex) know that those they cannot discipline can't live under their roof. I know this may sound harsh or even a little cold, but... it is something the husband must consider. As a parent, he may have to put his life on the line for that child. If he cannot discipline the child, how can he be expected to place his life on the line for them? The reason for disciplining is to protect the child, the family, and himself from danger. When danger occurs, there should be no second guessing on his reaction.

He may think about sitting down with the other parent (the ex) and getting to know each other. It may ease tensions he or both may have. It also involves his wife letting the children's father know she is getting married or has gotten married and what the rules of the new house are. All outside parents must be aware of the policies and their new role (greater or lesser) in those policies.

Teaching opportunities are endless. The husband should use this time to show the children what a man is and how he treats his kids and his wife. Every house can have a male, but only some may have men in them. All the boys in the house will determine the man they want to become based on him. Either they want to be like him or ...not. The girls in the house will also use him when picking a man for their lives. They may either choose to marry a man just like him or someone who is the opposite of him. He becomes the motivation in their future He must remember how important he is to them and their future.

Intimacy vs Sex

As a husband, learn and understand what sex is and what intimacy is. Knowing what goes where and why is good, but understanding when, when not, warm up, touching, holding, caressing, and even smiling is just as important. Maybe even more. Most men learn sex incorrectly through friends, family, magazines, movies, and even porn (he must be careful what he knows from porn. It really doesn't work out well). Many believe if they have an orgasm, he's good, and she is happy. The problem is she cared for him, but… did he take care of her?

Hmmm?

Understanding sex and how it applies to his wife is much easier if done the way God designed it. Yes, God created sex. He designed it to be passionate, full of life, excellent, invigorating, and beyond imagination. But sex has taken a turn in the way it is presented. In churches, it is, in my opinion, not discussed much, and when it is, it is sometimes viewed as a negative thing. Many have not read the Song of Solomon, how he and his bride romanced each other. The world, places outside the church, discuss sex in detail and as a good thing, especially when it is stolen.

Husbands must talk openly about sex with their wives, even when discussing and examining products. It takes the guessing game out of pleasing her and allows both to be more intimate and transparent, constantly seeking Godly ways to improve their relationship.

More and more people post pictures or stories of their sex lives for the world to see and celebrate. See the problem? God's people will not discuss something God made for them, even written in the Bible, but the world talks about it openly and freely. When couples discuss this matter, they are letting the world know being married does not destroy sex; it makes it much better, with so much freedom, love, and God.

Better sex starts with better intimacy, which leads to better sex. One way to achieve this is to discuss intimacy with her. Ask her essential questions such as what makes her melt in his arms, what makes her love to see him, and what he should do to turn her on. Ask her what works and what does not. Many husbands may not understand the questions, but their wives will.

Many women may give the same answers, meaning, as a husband, he may have heard them all before. However, the process of Initiating intimacy may differ. Why? He is the catalyst because he, the husband, is now involved. Once he has this information, he should use it.

Intimacy is touching in the mornings, kissing during the day, smiling, and holding hands in the car. Compliment her as much as possible on her body parts, legs, thighs, butt, breasts, smell, hair, nails, and dress. It is rubbing her feet, shoulders, and other things that will make her feel special. It is the phone call during the day to say I love you and think about you. I thank God for you as my wife.

Keeping sex great requires intimacy. Couples tend to let intimacy slip a little here, a little there, and then it is all but gone. Intimacy should be treasured, protected, and valued; engaged at every moment and in ways that help to improve it until it is at its best. Intimacy should feel natural, not forced. Holding, touching, or talking to his wife shouldn't feel tense or awkward. It shows that doing these things together is relaxing, exciting, and passionate.

Both husband and wife should welcome, appreciate, and desire intimacy. The husband should notice what makes his wife happy and be willing to work it into their lives.

I have heard couples grumble because one enjoys spending more time with friends than with their mates. Their solution is to stop the other from enjoying time with friends rather than seeing what they are doing and learning from it. One of my family friends got rid of their dog because the other was having more fun with it than with them. I suggested they notice what the dog was doing and mimic it.

Learn to laugh. Husbands must have a sense of humor. Please get a sense of humor and learn to enjoy life. He should recognize his wife's funny bone, even telling her jokes. When he enjoys life, it shows his wife that life is not as serious as many make it seem. He could also use this to show his faith in trusting a great God who will handle all his life issues.

A relationship without laughter is dying, or worse, already there. I have noticed couples on dates, and it appeared painful. Their stony facial expressions caused me to wonder when they forgot to laugh. When did life become so severe? It shows intimacy is damaged, and no one seems to care. Sex, for them, has probably become more like work, a chore, or just something to fulfill a need rather than how God designed it.

In a marriage, when sex and lust team up without intimacy, it could cause emotional problems; the wife may experience feelings of being used, not treasured, and not appreciated. Questioning if she has become "one of" than knowing she is the one. Husbands should do their best to ensure their wives never feel invaluable. Learn her body, her body language, her emotions, her moods, and ultimately her mind. She changes daily from the woman she was when she stood at the altar. She's maturing, not aging, but growing.

Remember that part. Husbands believing their wives know how they feel about them won't work; I am not sure it ever did.

Practice Self-Care

Husbands must practice self-care daily. Wives should not have to remind their husbands to shower or how to smell good. He should constantly smell good by putting on fragrances she likes that remind her of their intimacy.

Along with smelling good, he should dress better. Develop a look that represents your new family and will make them proud. Every time a husband leaves the house, he is a reflection of his wife as well as she is a reflection of him. When people look at him, they also look at his wife's husband (you) to represent her better, so she will be complimented on how great of a man she chose. It shows growth, responsibility, and maturity from boyhood to manhood.

Loving At the Door

Husbands meet her at the door as much as possible each time she comes home, especially from work. Have her call when she is close to home so she can be met at the door. There is more intimacy at the entrance of your home than in any other part of the house. She is welcomed home each time with a kiss, a touch, and questions on how her day went, and ongoing conversations continue in whatever part of the house she is going. Just talking.

He learns about her day and even helps her to undress and takes her bag, shoes, or coat. She gets pleasure from knowing her king is waiting for her. He becomes a joy to come home to, talk to, and her friend. When she is met at the door, give her a kiss that makes her toes curl, And her heart skips a beat and makes her fall in love again. A touch that makes her quiver just being close to you. Let her know she is a queen, your queen. The touching mentioned comes from the direction and guidance she allows. Ask her what touches she finds important. What touches mean most to her. What connects makes her feel special, and what touches makes her feel sexy, naughty, and desirable. Ask her what touches make her feel unappreciated or uncomfortable, and never do those. Notice we are talking about connecting, not groping, forcing, or taking…but touching. Touching her has a dynamic effect. It could lead to feeling appreciated, safe, comforted, protected, and… even loved. Remember, this is to learn how to touch her and allow her to feel special.

A significant part of touching is clean hands. The husband should always ensure his hands are clean when touching his wife, especially under his fingernails. Use a brush to get the grime and dirt from under those nails. This lets his wife know she is worth it; wives really appreciate it.

If a wife feels she is only touched for sex, this could be a problem. This is like someone happy to see you only when they want money. It may cause a setback in what she has overcome and learned to appreciate about herself; therefore, touching is essential. She must know she is touched because of love.

His wife should feel comfortable in her nakedness. She should feel like she could be vulnerable in her husband's presence. Can she walk in and vent to him? Can she cry on him or in front of him? Can he tenderly hold her without trying to solve the issue or tell her to suck it up, get a grip, and get over it? Can she tell him things she'd heard people say about her, and he not get angry and want to do something that could further damage her reputation? Can she always be herself with him?

Intimacy does not have a place or time. The husband may feel that he will be intimate with her when he gets home or goes out; you will do this or that. Intimacy can take place anytime and anywhere; it is an all-the-time thing. A simple phone call saying I was thinking about you and wanted to see how you are doing. You were on my mind, and I tried to call you and hear you smile. But, yes there is a but, you may feel your actions are not working. You are doing the things mentioned above and probably more, but you need help; what do you do now? Do you stop, give up, quit? What do you do? Through trial and error, what you may be doing is working. Unfortunately, you are looking for results without knowing the depth of the hurt she may have. Some hurt go deep. Each act of kindness brings her closer to the top and helps her conquer insecurities, hopefully, some of yours.

Intimacy is answering the phone when she calls. I have often seen men, or been in conversation with them, and their phone rings. They look at the screen and say, "Oh... it's just my wife; I will call her back later." Wrong move. They should have let her and everyone around know she is important. Answer her call. Tell her you are in a meeting or busy and will call her back. Ask her if she's okay, if anything is wrong, or if there is a problem. Asking these questions lets others know he's speaking with his wife, and she is more important to him than they are.

Now, he may ask, when does the sex part come in? Well, it already came in. It started when he started the intimacy work. When this work starts, his wife prepares herself to receive him. Her mind and body begin to lubricate themselves, making her ready to receive him in so many ways (Note: I am a man writing this, so don't quote me on the accuracy of this part). This is good because intimacy leads to sex, pleasurable sex, and sex where she is ready to receive and enjoy him. Now, they can reward one another through what God has given them... each other. If his wife has not lubricated herself or lost lubrication, sex can be stressful, painful, and not enjoyable. This is where many husbands say she is just not into sex. There are numerous reasons why his wife may lose lubrication. These could include menopause, his use of Viagra (for ego purposes) or other performance enhancement drugs, or he is demanding sex without giving her body time to react to foreplay or worse.

Let us talk about the drugs.

Just because the husband can go for hours (We all have heard the warnings of erections lasting longer than 3 hours) does not mean she can or will want to unless he finds ways to keep her lubricated and make it pleasurable for her. Wives could keep themselves lubricated, thinking of all the things they could or would be doing with their husbands. Therefore, intimacy works, is needed and desired.

Intimacy involves letting each other know what they like in the freaky side of their relationship. This is more difficult than he can imagine. Why is this so difficult? One reason is that communication has reduced or stopped. When he and his wife can talk about anything, then anything can be talked about. Communication is important, but it must be where they uplift each other and not put each other down. When names that tear each other down are thrown around, communication comes to a halt, causing feelings of unworthiness to begin and set in. This affects the way she wants to talk to him. She should be able to talk to him about anything crazy, stupid, funny, sad, or troubling.

This communication should not start the day he wants to have sex; it starts way before. If he has not started communicating this way, then now is a good time to start.

The Real Man

Have you ever heard the words real man used from time to time? People usually say if you were a real man, you would do this or would not have done that. Whatever THAT is. Wives have told their husbands they could not be good husbands (real men) because of their upbringing. But what is a real man, really? Does he have a standard, a position, a relationship? A certain amount of money, cars, or houses? Who is the example of a real man? What is his name?

Looking at the scriptures, only two real men ever existed, meaning they were perfect. The first actual man to ever live was Adam; yes, Adam was the first ideal man. The Bible never mentions a flaw in Adam. When God created him, he was perfect in all areas.

Then God gave Adam a woman, Eve, and they became imperfect.

Adam sinned when Eve gave him the fruit, and he freely ate it. Now, I'm choosing to tread lightly here. Many women want a real man, but they may do to that real man what Eve did to Adam. So, if he is concerned about being a real man, without flaws and perfect, forget it. None of us are perfect; he, the husband, never will be. So just be human. That's real enough. The second real man mentioned in the Bible is Jesus Christ in the flesh. No further comments are needed. Okay, maybe one. He never took a wife.

The concept of a real man is gaining speed as social media grows. People post more pictures and quotes of what real men do, say, or feel. They are usually posted by women. Are these real men or just men doing real things? Many women don't understand what they have done to deserve the type of man they're referencing. Can they handle a real man without trying to change him? If he is a real man, or better yet, a man being authentic, then he is not just a real man in his house; he is also a real man in his neighborhood, his community, with kids, with adults, and his Church, right? Others may also take notice of this man doing real things and want a real man. They desire HERS.

The definition of a real man should be a man who does real things, like following Proverbs 3:4-6. He trusts in the Lord with all his heart and leans not on his own understanding but in all his ways, he acknowledges God, and God directs his path. He also hides God's word so that he might not sin against God. Psalms 119. Being a real man may mean keeping his mouth closed when accused of not being real. He is not conforming to others' opinions but God's. He is standing firm in the face of insults.

Being a real man means realizing and accepting he is going to make mistakes, many of them. This is what real men do: make mistakes because they try and retry. They are not superheroes attempting to do unachievable or unrealistic things. They live on earth; they hurt, cry, succeed, and make mistakes. They look at the successes and mistakes of yesterday and learn from them, not dwell on them. They use their mistakes as teachers, not undertakers.

In becoming the man God created, be careful not to pick up the pressures of what the world wants or expects of him. He may forget he's human. Husbands become more aware of how things look to others and forget to live their lives. It's almost as if he believes he's a public figure seeking votes and beginning to live a phony life. Living as two people, one public and one private. Romans 3:23 reminds us of all who have sinned, messed up, and fallen short of the Glory of God. Notice the ALL.

Real men celebrate their wives as being proper, succeeding, and beautiful. They hold fast to their best ability to what is right. They love their kids and realize their greater goal is to raise Godly kids, not make millions or be successful businessmen. Being a successful Husband and Father is the best success he can have. Understand time is short and can never be returned; take advantage of it and enjoy each day as if it were his last. Real men do something we never see superheroes do: use the bathroom. So, if he ever forgets he's human, his bladder and bowels will remind him.

Doing Things Together, I Miss You

I spoke with a gentleman I know, and he mentioned something shocking and startling. He said that in his over 15-year relationship, which is ending, he can't think of anything he will miss that they did together. No sports, dinner, movies, hobbies, vacations (which they always fought about something), time with kids or even grandkids. I was stunned. I'm sure anyone would have been, but I didn't say anything. He saw my expression and confirmed nothing. Imagine that. Someone spends 15 years with their partner; when it is over, they miss nothing about them or their lives together. In my head, I was thinking of so many questions to ask but simply said EXPLAIN!

He said that, at first, we did things together. We took drives, rides, walks, and even had lunch and dinner dates. Then things changed slowly, but they changed. We drifted apart and got comfortable being apart from each other. We were too busy doing things alone or with other people to enjoy the other person's hobbies. We stopped teaching each other and accepted what we got. We argued more and touched less. Words of inspiration, support, and even love were given less and less. He said he tried, but the walls had become too strong and impenetrable.

Even the intimacy got less and soon died. He said he would come up with excuses allowing them to drive separately to the same places and events to avoid the awkward silence in the car. For him, being alone was better than being together. "Sad, isn't it?"

Husbands should do their best to participate in some of their wife's hobbies, maybe one or two. Wives should take part in some of their husband's hobbies as well. It is not for each other's enjoyment but for the sake of I miss you. Each husband should be missed by his wife when they are not together. Doing things together is not for the other to complain about but to enjoy the others' excitement in their hobby.

I spoke with a married couple while playing golf; she was in the cart, and he was playing. They informed me she does not play; she is just out here to support him, watch him, have fun, and laugh at him. One lady I spoke with was at the racetrack with her husband; I watched her as she read a book and enjoyed her time. She said she was not a big race fan, but her husband was, and she enjoyed watching him act like a big kid. I see couples at tailgate parties; the women are seated in a section while the men are in another. They were just out with each other, not complaining, arguing, demanding, or even being nasty; they were enjoying their love for each other.

When couples spend time with each other doing the other one's hobby, they are slowly creating an "I miss you moment." They are also making a best friend moment. I and my best friend went shopping, played sports, and or did dinner. We dated.

Creating these moments ensures that if the other does this alone, you are missed as their spouse, best friend, and cheerleader. Imagine them returning home and saying, I missed you out there today. It was not the same; no one cheered for me, high-fived me, laughed at me with a smirk, or kissed me. I missed you.

So, as a husband, do things together. When you drive, if possible, go together, open the door for her, pat her butt, and learn to talk. Do not use this time as an opportunity to complain, bicker, or share how smart you can be. Just take time to enjoy each other. Watch movies doing weird things, like under a blanket, on the floor, or in matching PJs. Just do something to let her know; I want you to miss me and miss me badly.

Sick and Tired of Being Sick and Tired

As there are so many marriages, there are just as many divorces. Unfortunately, these things happen, and I pray it does not happen to your marriage. I have shown, listed, and mentioned things meant to help husbands keep their marriage together in both beautiful and challenging times; however, marriage itself must be held together by at least two people: the husband, his wife, and, if possible, their families. Losing his relationship with God isn't worth the cost. A marriage should not and cannot be held together by one person. It won't work. It could lead to servitude, mistreatment, blame casting, and abuse. This abuse appears in many forms. There are many things to say about divorce, but here are a few. It hurts. No matter who says they are done first, initiates the filing, it will damage the couple and the families.

Divorce causes hurt. When husbands feel hurt by their mistakes, being wrong about who they selected as their partner, missing the red flags and warning signs, and not being loved as he feel he's loved. It also causes hurt knowing you must go back out on the dating scene. There is not enough time to discuss this part of life.

He will shed some tears as he goes through the process. It's ok. People will give him wanted and unsolicited advice on what he should or should not do.

How he should feel and not feel. Some people are caring and considerate, while others... not so much. Deep inside, they are not sad his relationship is ending.

Before he begins talking to others about his relationship ending or what caused it to end, sit down and have a long talk with God. Talk to God, the Comforter. Talk to God the Healer. Talk to God the Counselor. Talk to God the Creator. Talk to Him because the Doctor of healing must address the hurt. He can begin healing when he talks to God, reducing his hate and hurt feelings. The man draws closer to God, and realizes he is broken and needs a healer. He lowers the chances of trying to fix it on his own. This method rarely works well.

The benefits of talking to God first reduce, if not eliminate, the blame game. God already knows who to reward and who not to reward. The blame game is not just what he tells himself as much as what he tells others. The husband reduces the negative things they tell others about their relationship, wife, and family. He minimizes the lashing out because of the pain. Those words to other people won't stay with them but will cascade to others, and others and others. People will take sides in their relationship with or without inside information. Eventually, people will choose which side they take in their divorce. Divorce is personal, not private, but unique. It is not an opportunity to bad mouth the other or destroy their reputation. So please be careful with what information you share and with whom. This means helping others avoid what he went through to help them have a better marriage?

The first part of ending a marriage is the separation. This is the physical act that follows the emotional action. Both husband and wife began separating their emotions a while back. Now, they physically separate themselves one from the other. This is an emotional time, and the enemy will play havoc on each spiritually, emotionally, and mentally if they are not protected. There will be anger over material possessions, over new partners, over kids, if any, and over money. These things are designed to get him to take his eyes off God, place them on man, and fight for his rights.

He will hear stories about separations and divorce; some are good, but most are not. They speak of hurt, hate, anger, and even destruction. If he goes through this, remember that God has not left, deceived, or misled him. He is there with him, not playing games but loving him through, as a great Father does. Knowing this, be careful what he demands, fights for, or takes. This is what fuels so much anger and even hate. There will be times for name-calling, mudslinging, and smearing. Try to avoid this as much as possible. Remember, he is talking about the person he said he loves. What harm he does to her, he also does to himself.

www.ingramcontent.com/pod-product-compliance
Lightning Source LLC
LaVergne TN
LVHW051955060526
838201LV00059B/3660